Warrior

A play

Shirley Gee

Samuel French - London
New York - Toronto - Hollywood

WARRIOR

First presented by Chichester Festival Theatre in the Minerva Studio on 23rd June, 1989, with the following cast:

Hannah	Lois Harvey
Sculley	Tom Hollander
Mrs Sculley	Valerie Colgan
Susan	Victoria Scarborough
Godbolt	Chris Hunter
Drubber	Jonathan Drysdale
Billy Cuttle	Stanley Page
Flegg	Darren Tunstall
Ditch	Tom Hollander
Cumberland	Jonathan Drysdale
Dr Kemp	Darren Tunstall

Directed by Tim Luscombe
Designed by Paul Farnsworth

CHARACTERS

Hannah
Sculley
Mrs Sculley
Susan
Godbolt
Drubber
Billy Cuttle
Flegg
Ditch
Cumberland
Dr Kemp

Period: mid 1700s

Synopsis of Scenes

ACT I

The madhouse
Susan's house
The dockyard
The deck of the *Rainbow*
A small cove

ACT II

The madhouse
Susan's house
An ante-room
A dressing-room
On stage
The dressing-room
On stage
The dressing-room
On stage
The madhouse
The quayside

For Dan
*Whose rich imagination I have
so often plundered
with thanks and love*

AUTHOR'S NOTES

> Our Heroine has not her equal in any habitable Part of the
> World.
> (*The Female Soldier*—the life of Hannah Snell, 1750)

The real Hannah Snell was born in Worcester in 1723. She came to London,
and in 1744 married a Dutch sailor, James Summs, who left her seven
months' pregnant and ran off with her money back to sea. In November
1745, on the death of her infant daughter, Hannah, dressed in men's clothes,
set off in search of him. Taking her brother-in-law's name—James Grey—
she enlisted, and set sail aboard the *Swallow*.

> Says he, they're only taking him
> To the tender ship, you see.
> To the tender ship, cried Sally Brown,
> What a hardship that must be.
> (*Roxburghe Ballad*)

> You'll have nothing to do but sit and let the wind blow you
> along and live on plum pudding.
> (Recruiting Sergeant 1875)

For the next five years she lived and fought as a man. She survived storms,
leaky vessels, battles, expeditions, sieges, meagre rations, a lashing, and the
thousand ferocities aboard a man o' war—

> In war . . . every man must perform with a good grace. He must
> not bend his knees, nor hang his head, nor groan, nor tremble . . .
> (*The Marine Volunteer* 1766)

> I would give all I have if it was a hundred guineas if I could get
> on shore. We are looked on as a dog and not so good. Dear
> wife, make yourself as easy as you can. My ankles of my legs
> swell over my shoes . . .
> (Seaman's Letter 1800s)

—remaining buoyant, and undetected. In Lisbon, she had news at last of her
husband. James Summs, having killed a man in a brawl, had been
imprisoned and then flung in a sack into the sea. Seriously wounded in the
battle of Pondicherry, in the groin, she extracted the shot herself—

> In what Annals have we an Instance recorded of a Woman's
> choosing to die upon the Spot rather than have the Secret of her
> Sex revealed?
> (*The Female Soldier*)

In 1750 she sailed home, declared herself a woman, was finally given a pension and went on the stage, at the New Wells on a bill which included—

> Rope Dancing, Tumbling, Ladder Dancing, Surprising
> Exploits on the Slack Rope and Singing, all exhibited with
> great Decency and Decorum
> (*The Female Soldier*)

When the novelty for the public wore off, she opened a pub in Wapping called *The Widow In Masquerade*. Versions now get hazier; she remarried once, twice or not at all, she had two sons, one son, none. Certainly she died in Bethlem (Bedlam) in 1792, aged 69.

This is her life according to her Chap Book. It's a terrific read. Whether every word is true I wouldn't know. I take it with a pinch of sea salt here and there. I've taken some liberties, some small, some radical. I've changed her husband's name to Davey Snell. James Summs, James Grey and Hannah as James Grey—two James' in one play are a misfortune, three might seem like carelessness. I've lost her baby daughter—the death of a child is too heavy a matter to be sped over, and the story needed to race. The mind-reading act is an invention. So is everything which follows. The swing, however, was an approved treatment.

The most diabolical liberty is the "seeings". Nobody knows what sent her to the madhouse. Poverty, grief, disappointment in love? The horrors of war?

> What Fatigues, what Dangers must she run through ... when
> Bomb Shells and Cannons were displaying Death at every
> Moment. Reflections on such gloomy Occurrences as these are
> sufficient to shake the Temper of the most intrepid Soldier that
> ever appeared in battle, we may easily imagine that they must
> have had a stronger Influence over the female Mind.
> (*The Female Soldier*)

Disorientation caused by cross-dressing and notoriety?

> I no longer feel certain who I am or what others are—I feel as
> utterly isolated as anyone can be, and all links between myself
> and external objects, and between external objects and myself,
> have been broken.
> (Vesta Tilley—male impersonator 1900s)

Hallucination, delusion, obsession?

> Close and severe thinking has a direct tendency to weaken,
> confuse and destroy the intellect.
> (J. M. Cox *Practical Observations on Insanity* 1806)

> If a man comes in here mad, we'll keep him so. If he is in his
> senses, we'll drive him out of them.
> (John Mitford *Crimes and Horrors in the Interior of Warbur-
> ton's Private Madhouse* 1825)

I have pressed Hannah into my service, made her sail my troubled seas.
It's a shadow and a nightmare shared by many—

> In the event of a nuclear explosion—throw yourself at the wall
> nearest the explosion away from a window ... do not look at
> the explosion ... throw yourself into the shadows ... make
> yourself as small as possible ... do not move ... protect and
> brace yourself ... your sight will return in time ...
> (Tyrell *The Survival Option: A Guide to Living through Nuclear
> War* 1982)

> All things share the same breath—the beast, the tree, the man,
> they all share the same breath. This we know. The earth does
> not belong to man, man belongs to the earth. This we know.
> Whatever befalls the earth befalls the sons of the earth. Man
> did not weave the web of life; he is merely a strand in it.
> Whatever he does to the web, he does to himself ... Continue
> to contaminate your beds, and you will one night suffocate in
> your own waste.
> (Chief Seattle 1854)

My Hannah does not die in a madhouse. She fights on in her war against
wars. She and her comrades light up a dark world with their friendship,
love, endurance, courage. Let her have the last word.

> We recommend our Heroine to you as a Grand Pattern of
> Patience and Perseverance under the worst of Afflictions.
> Though the Clouds over our Head look ever so Black and
> Lowering, we may learn to live in Hopes that after the heaviest
> Storm there may come a Calm and the Sun, though for the
> Present obscured, may once more shine out in its Meridian
> Glory.

PRODUCTION AND DESIGN

The two central images of the play in terms of design are the mast and the swing. Both of these are practical, both permanent. The actors must be able to climb the rigging, but to protect Hannah it might be desirable to find a place on set for her to hide and fling a dummy in the swing.

Ideally the swing and the mast will be part of the same construction. Around it can be placed drums, ropes, flags, guns, barrels etc., to give character to the set without crowding it.

Whatever is needed for the duration of the play should be integrated into the set. This may mean that a single object can be used in different ways—e.g. a sail becomes a strait jacket, drums become barrels, a shovel becomes an oar, whatever.

The Union Jack should be permanently and prominently displayed.

It is vital that lengthy scene changes do not interrupt the forward surge of the play. It should flow continuously from one scene to the next. Sometimes a song may cover a change, sometimes trumpets and drums, or smoke and fire, or gaudy theatre lights or the furling and unfurling of banners or sails. Naturalism is not important, the style is tuppence coloured and vividness and colour should swirl throughout. In other words, while allowing quiet times for relationships to develop, the play should be as visually and aurally exciting as possible without slowing down its narrative flow, and the vibrancy and energy of the mid 1700s should be incorporated into the settings and costumes.

Warrior is in one giant flashback, bracketed by the madhouse scenes, until page 52, when the play catches up with itself and continues in a straight line until the end. There are eleven speaking parts and as many actors to drill, sing, climb the rigging, fill the madhouse and the theatre as you will. *Warrior* can also be played by a minimum of eight actors—three women, five men.

Miscellaneous
Physically the relationship between Hannah and Cuttle is one of easy comradeship. Hannah and Cumberland have a light affair in which both take pleasure though neither is emotionally involved. Between Hannah and Godbolt there runs a powerful high voltage sexual tension. By the end of the play, when their feelings for one another have deepened, Godbolt longs to speak, but his lips are stone. His heart is not. Not quite.

The mental magic scene (page 49) is an act—until Hannah's last apocalyptic vision overwhelms her. The verbal code required can be learned from

Annemann's *Practical Mental Magic* pp. 292/293. (Theodore Annermann. Pub. Dover 1983)

Hannah is not mad. She does not want to see into the future. Her "seeings" take an increasing physical and emotional toll as they increase in force and terror. When in the grip of them there is a still intensity, an urgency about her which commands attention. She is, of course, seen as quite insane. The threat of nuclear or chemical annihilation must have been unimaginable in the eighteenth century. It's hard enough to believe now.

The beat as an effect is something of a heartbeat, something of a drum, or a clock. Sometimes more like one than another.

Marching, the drums of war, drilling, digging, are in this rhythm, so almost subliminally it informs the whole.

The wind also threads throughout.

CHARACTERS

Hannah A visionary, a marine. Stubborn, passionate, fearful, brave, volatile, she is the magnet that draws all the characters in the play together. She makes a grand boy, but is entirely a woman. Her accent need not be strong, but should have a roughened edge.

Sculley Madhouse keeper. Gets a morose enjoyment from his distressing work. Unimaginative rather than cruel. Has an eye on the main chance.

Mrs Sculley His wife. Madhouse attendant. Coarse-grained, capable, tough and kindly.

Susan Hannah's sister-in-law. Worn, impatient, sensible. Her life is a hard struggle. Cross and loving.

Godbolt Sergeant of Marines. A hard man. Dark and haunted. A superb soldier, his word is law. His men may resent him but their trust in him is absolute; if anyone can get them home in one piece, he can. Moral, loyal, upright, frozen. He walks alone.

Drubber A marine. A swaggerer, a bully. Physically strong. Superstitious. Alarming. Second in command. Young.

Cuttle A marine. Older. A good man. Simple, but not a buffoon. Easy to kick, but gains strength through his friendship with Hannah.

Flegg A marine. Older. A seasoned campaigner. Knows how to work the system. Fatherly. Wry.

Ditch A marine. Younger. Drubber's disciple, but a puppy, excitable, easily swayed.

Cumberland An aristocrat. Attractive. Far too powerful a man to have to raise his voice. Moves through all strata of society with careless assurance and ease. A hedonist. Dangerous to cross. His delight in Hannah is genuine.

Dr Kemp The madhouse doctor. A grave, kind, moderate, professional man. Played with compassion and concern it makes Hannah's dilemma more dreadful.

The action of the play takes place in the mid seventeen hundreds.

ACT I

The madhouse

Hannah in a harsh light, in a night-shift

Hannah I cannot . . . I must . . . they come into my mind. They say tell about me. Tell when the shadows lengthened on the grass, when the shadows— NO! The wind lifts the blossom, the wind blows, like it always blows, on all of us. (*She sings*)

> Now I went out to walk one day,
> The wind was rather strong that way,
> In fact it blew the lot away . . .

(*Speaking*) Ten . . . nine . . . eight . . . seven . . . six . . . five . . . four . . . (*She screams*)

The Lights come up on stage. Two attendants, Sculley and Mrs Sculley are with her. Mrs Sculley holds Hannah, roughly but not unkindly. Sculley pauses in oiling the swing, a large, heavy contraption rather like a see-saw with a chair in which the patient is strapped at one end, a weight at the other.

Sculley A penny a time to see the raving. (*He holds his cap out to the audience*) A penny to see them cured. (*He laughs, turns back to work*)

Mrs Sculley pulls off Hannah's shift, scrubs her down with a long-handled mop, as you might an elephant at the zoo

There's all sorts here. Cholerics. Melancholics. Hysterics. (*Turning to Hannah*) Which are you?

Mrs Sculley To be seen and enjoyed and lessons learned and a good day's outing.

Sculley Brutes, some of 'em. Brutes. And some is stones.

Mrs Sculley She's not, though. Are you, lovie? Not a brute and not a stone. Just her brain's gone topsy–turvy.

Sculley The brain's a noble organ.

Mrs Sculley It is, it is. Lords it over the rest of the body. But when it goes topsy-turvy—well.

Sculley What was it, now, as made her lunatic? Drink was it?

Mrs Sculley Or grief. (*She taps Hannah's foot*) Lift.

Hannah lifts her foot, Mrs Sculley turns to the audience

See? She's not unmanageable, like some. (*Scrubbing*) I'll put my penny on disappointment in love. (*She taps Hannah's other leg*) T'other.

Hannah lifts it

Sculley Whatever it is, bodily disorder, poverty, a sudden change in fortune, he'll seek out the cause. The doctor, he'll dig and he'll dig until he finds it.

Mrs Sculley He's wonderfully fond of causes. He's in high hopes of restoring her. (*Now drying Hannah, putting her shift back on*) But if he can't—this is your last chance.

Sculley If he can't——

Sculley has finished oiling the swing. He pats it. Hannah stiffens, stares at it. Sculley laughs

—she'll fly like a bird.

Hannah tries to run, but Mrs Sculley holds her

All the same when you face them with the swing.

Mrs Sculley You'll be all right. You can be cheerful for a long space of time, I've seen you. Be respectful. Answer him loud and clear. What's your name . . . ?

Hannah Hannah. Hannah Snell.

Mrs Sculley How's that for an answer? How old are you, Hannah?

Hannah Thirty-one.

Mrs Sculley See. Lucid as any.

Hannah Hannah Snell.

Mrs Sculley Born in the year of our Lord . . .

Hannah Seventeen hundred and twenty-three, in the city of Worcester. Moved to London, seventeen hundred and thirty-five. Married David Snell, sailor . . . oh, Davey . . .

Mrs Sculley Hold fast to your wits, dearie. Married David Snell, sailor . . .

Hannah On a foggy day in January seventeen hundred and forty-four. A lovely lad, and a scoundrel. Oh, Davey . . .

Susan's house

Hannah (*a scream*) DAVEY!

The Sculleys retire

Hannah, aged eighteen or so, stands alone, in her nightshift. She holds a letter

Oh, no. DAVEY!

Susan enters, startled out of sleep

Oh, Susan.

She holds out the letter. Susan takes it

Susan "Dear one. I'm not meant to be stuck ashore. I've signed back on the *Cloud*." The dog. "Sorry about the two pound. Never fear. I'll come back rich as a king, your loving Davey." The double dog. Gambling again?

Hannah He promised me. He swore.

Susan He'd eat a live cat for a wager. Two pound?

Hannah A bit above.

Susan How in God's earth will you find two pound?

Hannah I don't know, do I? I'd pledge the spoons, but there's no spoons left to pledge.

Susan You've nothing?

Hannah Less than nothing.

Susan Well, I'm sorry Hannah, but I have to say it. You've dug your own pit. Always a shilling behind, that's you. What'll you do? They'll come after you. They will. It'll be prison, Hannah.

Hannah (*looking round wildly*) There's the clock. That's ours. And ... and ... (*she can't see anything else*) and ... (*She takes off her locket*)

Susan Six shillings. Seven at most.

Hannah What'll I do? I don't know what to do.

Susan No use looking to me and Caleb, we can't help.

Hannah Course not. We're living on you as it is.

Susan Not that we grudge you, mind. After all, he is my brother. Even if he is the back end of a dog. And you're a good soul, Hannah.

Hannah Lord, I'm afraid of prison.

Susan Cassie Terson cut her throat because her husband ran off with her savings. Whatever will you do?

Hannah When he comes back I'll crack his head for him so hard.

Susan Comes back? He's forgotten you already.

Hannah Never.

Susan Did he tell you he was going?

Hannah No.

Susan Well then.

Hannah I think he tried. He cried in my arms last night.

Susan Well he might.

Hannah I can feel his tears on the back of my hand.

Susan Without your man you're nothing. Lost your place.

Hannah staggers suddenly, covers her eyes with her hands a moment, takes her hands away, stares

What is it? What——?

Hannah The sea. The sea. It's everywhere.

Susan Oh my Lord.

Hannah There's Davey standing in it, at the edge. He's staring at me. Oh, his eyes are sad. Now his shadow's left him ... and turned white ... and sank beneath the waves.

Susan I hate it when you're like this.

Hannah There's blood in the sea. Drops of blood, like ladybirds, on him. He's sinking now. He's gone.

Susan Oh, Hannah, you do frighten me.

Hannah dives suddenly for a clothes chest, starts to haul clothes out

What are you doing now?

Hannah Going after him. He'll drown. I have to stop him.

Susan You can't. Hannah, you can't.

Hannah is pulling on a shirt

It's only a dream

Hannah I don't dream. I see.

Susan (*of the shirt*) That's Caleb's.

Hannah He'll get it back.

Susan It's his best.

Hannah It's not. It's the other one. (*Tugging on long johns*) You know it's a warning. Remember the bolting horse? And the fire? And the night your father died? I saw them all. He mustn't go to sea.

As Susan starts to speak

I know. They're Caleb's too. I'd have worn Davey's but he's took them all.

Susan Let him go. He's worthless.

Hannah He's good at heart.

Susan All because of some stupid, stupid dream——

Hannah Do you want the sea to have him? (*She puts on shoes and stockings*)

Susan You never stop to think. He's had the night's start. What if he's sailed already?

Hannah Then I'll go to sea as a sailor. Follow him.

Susan You don't know anything about the sea.

Hannah The sea is blue. And deep.

Susan And you've to watch it for it's after you to pull you down.

Hannah I've learnt to make a soup and light a fire and pledge a thing I haven't got. (*Cramming hair into a cap*) I'll soon get used to it.

Susan Sailors are demons.

Hannah Davey's a sailor.

Susan They live in sin and blood. And die in it. What if you get swept up in a war?

Hannah (*dressed now*) How'll I do?

Susan You wouldn't fool a rabbit.

Hannah Is it here? (*Her breasts*)

Susan It's all of you. Anyone could tell with half an eye.

Hannah I do swell, don't I. (*She rushes to the chest, pulls out a long piece of cloth, takes off her shirt, wraps it round*) Tie it. Oh, quick, Suke. Please.

Susan ties the cloth tight

I can't be a man, but I can be a boy.

Susan Man or boy, you'll have to breathe. How do you think you're going to manage among all those men?

Hannah I'll snarl and spit and march about a bit. (*Dressed again, she rolls a seaman's sock of Davey's, uses it for a codpiece*) How's that?

Susan Better. Much. How'll you do at night?

Hannah Snore. Belch. Fart. I shall fart all night if I want.

Susan Hannah, you can't.

Hannah I can do anything. Once you're a man you can kick the world like a king. (*She collects a few things—a mug, candles, matches, a knife, bundles them into a man's jacket*)

Susan You're determined, then?

Hannah Like iron. Don't worry, Suke. Soon as he sees me, he'll come back.
Susan You must be careful.
Hannah I will.
Susan (*crying*) You mustn't cry, no matter what.
Hannah (*not crying*) I won't.
Susan You must be gruff.
Hannah (*gruff*) I will.
Susan Better still, be silent.

Hannah nods

And grim.

Hannah nods grimly

You are the best ... the ... stupidest sister-in-law a body could ever ... If anyone finds you out ... oh, feel my heart. Leave it a week and see.
Hannah I can't. How can I? (*She sees Davey's kerchief sticking out of his trousers pocket, pulls it out, is sad. She recovers, and ties it round her neck*) I'll find him and I'll bring him back and there's my mind and there's the end of it. (*She marches upstage, turns*) The sea shan't have him. (*She salutes*) Everything strong and hearty.
Susan (*calling after her as she goes*) Hannah! You're off to the slaughter-house.
Hannah Not I. I'll sail like the moon in the sky.

Susan exits

As Hannah crosses and recrosses the stage she becomes more confident, more at home in her clothes. She kicks at stones, tries to whistle, fails, succeeds at last and is delighted with herself. She exits

The dockyard

A roll of drums. Godbolt and Drubber drum up recruits

Godbolt Roll up, roll up for the good life, lads. The good rich life. A gallon of beer a day. A bountiful supply of clothing, the ladies flocking and the rest of your life in peace and plenty.
Drubber Go the world over. See the Hanging Gardens of Babylon——

Cuttle bursts in, breathless. A man, not a boy

Cuttle I'm here.
Drubber The yellow men of China, the monsters of the deep blue sea——
Cuttle I'm game, sirs.
Drubber Chase the Frenchie fleet across the seas——
Cuttle By Christ I'll chase them off, whoever they are, the more the merrier——
Godbolt Welcome my fine sir. Name?
Cuttle Cuttle, sir. Billy Cuttle, sir.
Godbolt Mister Cuttle, sir.
Drubber (*aside*) Seems a bit of a dung barge.

Cuttle Here, sir, at His Majesty's service.

Godbolt (*to Cuttle*) A likely man indeed. (*Aside*) The Navy needs warm bodies.

Cuttle I'm game for anything, by hell I am.

Drubber (*to Godbolt*) He stinks of jail to me.

Hannah enters

Hannah Excuse me——

Drubber (*crossing to her, pulling her forward*) Now this looks a tall enough boy.

Hannah Excuse me. Can any man here tell me——

Drubber Holds himself smart enough.

Godbolt Good. Good. Come to the aid of your country like an Englishman.

Hannah No. Indeed no. I'm looking for a mate of mine. Shipmate. Name of Snell.

They shake their heads

Davey Snell.

They shake their heads

He signed aboard the *Cloud*.

Godbolt (*pointing to a board*) The listings are all there. I think you'll find you've missed him.

Hannah Missed him!

Godbolt Here, I'll read it for you.

Hannah Thank you. Thank you.

Godbolt Never mention it. A man must help another. (*He blocks the board from Hannah's sight, surreptitiously wipes out some of the names scrawled there in chalk*) The *Cloud*. Sailed on the morning tide. Next port of call Lisbon.

Hannah Oh no. When's the next merchantman?

Godbolt The *Swallow*. Docked for repairs. The *Calico* ... sailed last week. The *Lady Mary* ... The *Drum* ... No luck, lad. There's none. No sailings for a week.

Hannah What'll I do?

Godbolt Looks like you're out of luck.

Hannah He's my ... my sweetheart's brother. I must find him. Bring him back.

Godbolt I can see it means a deal to you. What can we do to help this gentleman, Drubber? Tell you what, we're Lisbon bound, you could follow him with us.

Drubber That's it. Catch him up, and on the way see all the lands that's over the water.

Godbolt Hear the silver chink of a shilling a day.

Cuttle Oh sirs both, just let me at 'em.

Godbolt You still here?

Hannah I can't enlist. A merchantman, yes, but ...

Godbolt Give all you've got to get at the enemy of your country?

Hannah Yes, but . . .
Drubber Come back with a Frenchie's ear?

Hannah nods

   Not womanish are you?

She shakes her head

Godbolt If you want to find your Davey Snell, it's us or nothing. Name?
Hannah James. James Grey.

Drubber seizes her, forces her mouth open

Drubber All his own teeth. Must have your own teeth to bite your cartridge.
   (*He shakes her, tosses her to Godbolt*) See that, Sergeant? Free motion of
   every joint——
Godbolt (*flinging her back to Drubber*) Limbs nice and easy——
Drubber Seems like a proper specimen, Sergeant Godbolt.
Godbolt Very proper, Mister Drubber. (*He catches her, spinning her round
   the other way*)

Hannah staggers, dazed. Drubber holds up both hands

Drubber How many hands do I hold up?
Hannah (*gasping*) Two.

Drubber lets off a musket shot

Godbolt Can you hear that, lad?

Deafened, hands over ears, she nods

Drubber He's the proper use of his eyes and ears.
Godbolt In every respect fit for His Majesty's service. Sign, sir, sign for the
   Rainbow.

Hannah, still dazed, nods

Cuttle And me, sirs. I'll sign. I saw the two hands, clear. I heard the shot.
   My limbs is free.
Godbolt (*aside*) This one's a muckfly. (*To Cuttle*) Sign, then.

He pushes the book to Cuttle, who signs

Cuttle There's only been but one path before me, sir. At your side sir.
Godbolt Depresses me to hear you say that.
Cuttle I'll fight so fair and I'll sail so sweet——
Drubber (*rolling his drum*) Billy Cuttle, James Grey, from henceforth in
   God's and the King's eyes you are a Christian and a Marine. (*He rolls the
   drums*)

Drubber and Godbolt start to go

Godbolt (*as they go*) Roll up, roll up for the good life, the good rich life. Sail
   the Black sea and the Red sea and the Yellow sea. Spend the rest of your
   life in peace and plenty . . .

Drubber and Godbolt exit

Hannah What do I know of soldiers?

Cuttle Their coats are red. They march over hills.

Hannah And guns are loud. And a ball can kill. Oh Lord, I've done it now.

Cuttle Ay, sir. That's done all right. You've done it and so have I and all the saints up in the sky cannot undo it.

Hannah on one side of the stage, Cuttle on the other, are kitted out. Shirt, shoes, waistcoat, britches, coat, hat, bedding. They change into uniform. Cuttle is proud, delighting in his new clothes, looking ramshackle as ever. Hannah is in panic

Hannah What have I done?

Drubber passes with a load of muskets

Hannah, undressed, freezes, arms crossed over her breasts, until he's gone

Drubber exits

Lord, I'm alone.

Ditch and Flegg cross, look at her

She hurries to get dressed

They amble off

I don't know one end of a musket from the other.

Cuttle is dressed. Drums. Hannah marches to join the others. Cuttle follows, stumbles

The deck of the "Rainbow"

Hannah, Cuttle, Flegg, Ditch and Drubber stand to attention in line

Hannah (*out of the side of her mouth*) Why don't we sail tonight?

Godbolt What's that?

Hannah I must sail, Sergeant. I've lost six days already. When do we sail?

Godbolt We sail, Grey, when you, Grey, have learned the rudiments. So that you, Grey, do not die like a rotten sheep and inconvenience the Navy. Understand? Today we master the art of prime and load. (*Demonstrating*) To prime and load. Twenty-one motions. First. Recover your firelock.

They do. The weapons are immensely heavy. Hannah almost drops hers. Short silence

Your musket is your girl. You oil her, polish her, wrap her in flannel. You can find her in the dark, you sleep with her. YOU DO NOT DROP HER. Anyone who drops his musket, he'll feel blood run over his nose.

Hannah Ay, Sergeant.

Godbolt Second. Pose.

They do

Third. Cock your firelock.

They do

Listen with particular care. Stepping back with the right foot—the right foot, Cuttle you slug-brain—four inches behind the left heel, and facing full to the right—the left hand half-way between the swell and the feather spring, spring back the butt of the rifle, the lock just above the right breast, the left arm pressed against the body so as to support the piece——

Hannah staggers, recovers

—the muzzle of which is to be raised as high as the man's head in the rank before you . . .

Cuttle's musket wavers, slowly sinks. Godbolt watches. The barrel touches the ground. Cuttle gradually sinks with it, kneels

Prayer won't help you. Get up, you idle slumping pisspot.

Cuttle still holding his musket, struggles to rise. Hannah steps forward to help him

Cuttle's nursemaid, are you?
Hannah No, Sergeant.
Godbolt Want to hold his hand?
Hannah No, but I thought——
Godbolt It's your duty not to think. You're lamentable, Grey. I feel queasy when I look at you. You're like some pissing sea lily. What are you?
Hannah A sea lily.
Godbolt A pissing sea lily. Sergeant.
Hannah A pissing sea lily. Sergeant.
Godbolt Who's going to nursemaid you? Eh? Who's going to hold your hand?

Hannah stands for a moment frozen. Isolated. Shocked. Around her is tremendous activity. Ropes fly across the stage, to be caught or coiled or hooked or flung back again. A man climbs. Two men haul on ropes. They sing as they pull

All (*singing*)   A long haul for Widow Skinner
                   Cheerly men
                   Kiss her well before dinner
                   Cheerly men
                   At her boys and win her
                   Cheerly cheerly cheerly o.

Hannah, still alone, takes Davey's handkerchief from her pocket. She misses him

                   A strong pull for Mrs Bell
                   Cheerly men
                   Who likes a lark right well
                   Cheerly men
                   And what's more will never tell
                   Cheerly cheerly cheerly o.

Hannah pulls herself together, joins the others, pulls on the ropes. A great sail starts to rise, billows

> A haul and split the blocks
> Cheerly men
> A haul and stretch her luff
> Cheerly men
> Young lovelies, sweat her up
> Cheerly men
> Cheerly cheerly cheerly o.

Godbolt Up helm. LET EVERYTHING FLY!

The sail balloons, cracks. It's up. A cheer goes up

> *The crew rush off in different directions to go about their tasks*

Hannah is left with Godbolt, on deck, seasick

Aboard the "Rainbow"

Godbolt comes up behind her. Grabs her hair, forces her to look out over the sea

Godbolt See that you snotty boy?
Hannah Yes, Sergeant. What, Sergeant?
Godbolt The sea, you godless ninny.
Hannah OW! Yes, Sergeant. I see it, Sergeant.
Godbolt It's all about us. Heaving. Boiling. Endless. Two hundred and ninety nights in a hammock when the cold wind freezes you. When the hot sun softens your pitch. A pissing sea lily won't last two weeks. (*He flings her away, turns to go, stops, turns back again, stares at her*) You all present and correct?
Hannah Sergeant.
Godbolt Got a pair of bollocks?
Hannah Oh. Er. Yes, Sergeant. Yes indeed.
Godbolt Let's see 'em. Get up that mast and reef the topsail. I want to see 'em. Flegg!

Hannah stands paralysed

> You got ears?

She nods

> Flegg! If you ears don't function in the proper regulation manner I'll lop 'em off. Up aloft.

Flegg enters

> See this man up, Flegg
Flegg Ay ay, Sergeant.
Godbolt See it done. I'll be back, Grey. (*He starts to go. At the last moment he turns*) There's more than ears I long to lop off. Understand?

Hannah, gazing up at the mast, nods

See it done.

Godbolt leaves

Hannah stares up

Flegg Three things a man can never say at sea. I can't. I won't. I am afraid.
Hannah Oh God.
Flegg You can think it, but you can't say it.
Hannah Marines don't have to go aloft. The Articles——
Flegg Don't waste your breath. You'll need it. Want my help?

Hannah nods

Face the sea. A sailor has his back to the land, his face to the sea, he's born that way. Face it. Stare it out.

She does

Can you stand straight?
Hannah I think so.
Flegg Stand straight. Breath deep. Feel the sea in your bones. Are you steady?
Hannah Ay.
Flegg You look steady. Go on, then.

Hannah goes to the mast, clasps it firmly, bravely, looks up and almost faints

Use your hands, son. Two feet one hand for yourself, one hand for your country.

She starts to climb. A few feet up she is terrified again, can't move. Flegg takes an oar, beats her repeatedly behind the knees, forcing her up

Go on. Get on. You're all right. More like to die washed off the jib boom. Go on there. Get on.

She climbs on. Slow, sick, fearful

Roll with the breakers.

She looks down, up. Terror either way

He'll have you down below in irons. He'll have you stripped.

That sends her up

Use your fear, son. Make a friend of it. It's old hands fall off the rigging. They get careless. Forget to be afraid.

She's out of sight

Are you there?
Hannah (*calling down*) Ay.
Flegg How is it?
Hannah (*calling down*) Cold.

Flegg Reef the topsail?
Hannah (*calling down*) Ay ay.

Flapping and cracking. Shouts from Hannah. Then calm

  Godbolt returns

Flegg Topsails reefed, Sergeant.

Godbolt nods, turns to go

Hannah (*calling down*) I'm here, I'm aloft, I've done it, Sergeant, look
  I've——
Godbolt (*calling up*) Understand this, Grey. I'll say it once and only once. In
  my world and on my ship and in this war we're off to fight—if you haven't
  got bollocks you'll be nothing but a stench in the wind before you grow a
  beard.

  He exits. When he's gone . . .

Hannah (*calling down*) Poxy bastard. (*She climbs down*)

  Cuttle and Ditch return

  Oh, Flegg, you can see everything there ever was up there. I've just been
  up, Ditch. The shrouds just came into my hands. Cuttle, I've just——
Flegg Be shaving next.
Ditch Shaving off his whisker. Save it for us, Jem.
Flegg Put it under glass.
Ditch Be fair, Flegg, be fair. He's got two. The other's on his chest. Show
  us. (*He lunges at her*)
Hannah Get off, Ditch.
Ditch Girlish, ain't he. Show us your martial chest.

A menacing moment, broken by . . .

  The arrival of Drubber with rations—beer, beef and biscuits

*They turn their attention to him hungrily as he shares out. Ditch holds out his
biscuit to Flegg*

Flegg Maggots.
Cuttle I got them too. Mine's waving their heads about.

Drubber hands her a biscuit

  Ugh!
Ditch The meat's shifting. Can't hardly hold your head over it.
Cuttle (*spitting out his beer*) Goat's piss. Can't ask a man to fight on this.
Ditch I'll not stand for it.
Flegg Nor me.
Hannah Nor me neither. One of us must tell him.

All look at Drubber

Drubber Not me.

Flegg It's your place.
Ditch You're his man.
Drubber Not me, I said.

A silence

Cuttle Where'd you get your dinner, Drubber? That good bread?
Drubber That's my business.
Cuttle Know what I'm wondering? What I'm wondering is, how is it we get
   dead beer and beef like horse and you get bread and pork and lemons.
Drubber You idle lumping toad.
Cuttle Have my biscuit. Look. It's creeping.
Drubber A maggot here and there'll do no harm.
Hannah There's hundreds of them, Drubber.
Drubber What won't poison you'll fatten you.
Cuttle Our meat stinks wicked.
Drubber Think of nothing but your belly, Cuttle?
Cuttle Yours don't, though, do it. And our beer stinks, too.
Drubber Know what happens, Cuttle, to a man who loves his belly above all
   else? Above his King? Above his God? Above his duty?
Cuttle I hope I know my duty. And I know for every one of us lost, there's
   ten of us dies from bad provisions.
Drubber You dog.
Cuttle I don't think the King wants us to starve while you gets pork and
   greens.
Drubber You whoring dog.

Drubber strikes Cuttle hard with his club. Cuttle falls

   This is a stick of barley sugar compared to what's coming to you. All or
   any of you. One more word you'll have your dinner at the bottom of the
   sea. Greed is a sin, you shag-brained gutter-dogs. So's wastefulness at sea.
   I see a crumb down by my boot. Whose crumbs are those?
Cuttle Yours, Drubber. From your bread.

Drubber clouts Cuttle

Drubber Anyone else think they're mine?

A silence

   Spoil the whiteness of the deck. Sergeant Godbolt's very particular about
   the whiteness of his deck. Ain't he, lads.

A murmur of "Yes Drubber" from the crew

   Yes, Drubber. They're Cuttle's crumbs, ain't they, Ditch?
Ditch Yes, Drubber.
Drubber Cuttle's crumbs, Grey?
Hannah Yes, Drubber.
Drubber Yes, Drubber. Right.

Drubber thuds into Cuttle again, throws Hannah a broom

Clap on to this. Bucket. Sand. Clean up this mess.

Ditch and Flegg go for water and sand. As Cuttle tries to rise ...

Stay on your knees and holystone the deck.

He exits

The crew cluster round Cuttle

Flegg Made a hog's arse out of that, Cuttle.
Hannah He'll never go to Godbolt now.
Ditch (*kicking him*) Lost our chance for us, you par-boiled cod.
Cuttle Leave me alone.
Ditch Because of you we're to go on as we are. Foul meat. (*Kick*) Salt fish.
   (*Kick*)

Flegg has fetched the holystone. A white prayer-book shaped stone used for whitening the deck

Get on with it.
Flegg What did you have to bring the King into it for? (*He kicks him*)
Ditch Hear my sides clap together?
Hannah Ay. (*She kicks the stone out of his reach*)
Cuttle (*who has been trying to scrub under the onslaught*) I tried what I
   could.

They kick the stone to one another Cuttle scrabbles after it on his knees

You're bad lads, all of you.
Ditch Muckfly. (*Hitting him*) We're to starve. Because of you. (*He hits him on the head*) Because of you. (*Again*)
Cuttle (*trying to rise*) I'm one of you.

Drubber returns

Drubber (*hitting him*) Stay on your knees.

Cuttle scrubs. Drubber hits him

Advance.
Cuttle For God's sake, Drubber. I can't hardly see.
Drubber ADVANCE!

Cuttle shuffles forward blindly. Scrubs. He is now bleeding

Cuttle. You are spilling blood upon the deck. You have defiled His
Majesty's forecastle.

Cuttle swabs at the blood as hard as he can

Bleeding on the holystone. That's blasphemy. That's for the captain.
That's a hanging matter.

Cuttle staggers up. Drubber picks up a bucket of water

First better swill the stench off him.

The others collect buckets, stand in a half circle. Cuttle, bleeding, cowers. He tries to face them. Suddenly Hannah, broom in hand, leaves the group and stands in front of Cuttle

Hannah NO!

Drubber Out of the way, Grey.

Hannah Leave him alone.

Flegg Keep out of it, Jem.

Hannah No-one's to touch him.

Ditch What's up with you. You lammed in as hard as us.

Hannah I did, and I'm ashamed. He did his best.

Drubber lunges at her. She wields the broom in a wide arc—he can't get near

What makes you so cruel, Drubber?

Drubber I'm authorized. I have my duty.

Hannah One step—

Drubber Look at you. Swan on a lake.

Hannah One step and I'll pour you over the side like the pisspot you are.

Drubber I'll roll you round the deck like a bottle. With one hand. (*He snatches an oar, raises it high to smash down on Cuttle*)

Hannah NO! No, Drubber. STOP!

A wind blows mournfully

Your heart——(*She staggers, covers her eyes a moment, takes her hands away, trembling*) Your heart. It's come out of your mouth.

Drubber Eh? What's he saying?

Hannah There. (*Pointing*) Dark. Big as a fist. (*Watching as it hovers*) Dripping on the deck.

All stare at her in silence

It's going. Sinking into the sea.

The wind fades

Gone.

Drubber Jesus holy Christ.

A silence

Flegg I seen him have a turn like this before. The night old Shemp fell from the mizzen shrouds.

Ditch You're for it, Drubber.

Drubber Me? Not me.

Ditch Your heart come out of your mouth.

Drubber (*turning on Hannah*) Think to catch me with a trick like that? Damn your eyes and damn your visions.

Godbolt is heard, off

Wait till I tell him.

Hannah (*quickly, slightly theatrical*) I see a dark bird following the wake. Hovering above you now. Come for your soul, Drubber.

Flegg and Ditch back away

Ditch What are you? The devil?

Hannah Don't mix with what you don't know. Hook it.

Ditch backs further. Flegg and Drubber transfixed, cross themselves

Get your carcasses out of my sight. All of you. HOOK IT!

Drubber You can go hang, Grey.

They exit

Hannah and Cuttle watch them go in silence, smile at one another. Hannah wrings out her kerchief in a bucket, bathes Cuttle's wounds

Cuttle Anything you ever want, sir. Anything. Billy Cuttle's your man.

Hannah Thanks, Billy.

Cuttle Thank YOU, sir. You told 'em, sir. Them deck planks smoked beneath your feet. Fair shook me.

Hannah Shook me. I'm shaking still. First time I've ever stood up for myself. Ever. Let's see your back.

Cuttle (*taking off his shirt*) Not much left of it, sir.

Hannah God's teeth.

Cuttle I seem to bring out the feelings in everyone, sir.

Hannah You shouldn't call me sir. I'm not an officer.

Cuttle You're a gentleman, sir, to me. There's no-one ever spoke up for me before. I'll stick to you, sir, like tar to your trousers.

A call from Godbolt off. Cuttle puts his shirt back on. Both scrub frantically

Lord, he'll have me splintered. He knows how to make the rope find your liver. If Drubber tells on you——

Hannah He won't.

Cuttle You saw that heart all right, but not the bird. Am I right?

Hannah You are.

Cuttle You're a man in a thousand, sir.

Hannah I am.

Cuttle Luck and me don't march together much. But if you'll have me, sir, I'm yours. Bone to bone. Shadow to shadow.

The wind blows. A throbbing beat begins

Hannah Bone to bone. Shadow to shadow.

They clasp hands. Freeze a beat. The stage darkens

The sail slowly sinks down. The wind blows hard, then fades. The beat continues behind

A huge drum roll. Cuttle and Hannah are joined by the rest, who gather, listen. Godbolt climbs the rigging. The Lights are up

Godbolt Men. In the morning we meet our enemy. We must sweep them off the seas. These seas are British seas. There's British fish in them. The East Indies is part of the British Empire. The British flag floats over it, bringing with it justice, order, prosperity, and the Christian religion. The greedy Frenchies want to grab it from us. Their eagle's bloody claws are spread to hook into our wine, our silks and spices, your tea and sugar and tobacco. When the wealth of the Colonies is threatened, the Empire itself is threatened. He who'd be secure on land must be secure at sea. THE KING NEEDS THE SEAS. Men. We fight for two glorious causes. LIBERTY!

All cheer

AND PROPERTY!

All cheer

GOD SAVE THE KING!

The drums roll mightily, die away. The stage darkens as the men prepare for battle. As they do, Ditch sings, the rest join in the chorus

Ditch (*singing*)	When I was young and in my prime
	I thought I'd go and join the line
	And as a soldier cut a shine
	In a lot called the hungry army.
Chorus	Sound the bugle, blow the horn
	Fight for glory night and morn
	Hungry soldiers, ragged and torn
	Just returned from the army.
Ditch	They cut my hair with a knife and fork
	And curled it with a cabbage stalk
	They fed me up on cabbage broth
	To fight in the hungry army.
Chorus	Sound the bugle, blow the horn . . . *etc.*
Ditch	Now I went out to drill one day
	The wind was rather strong that way
	In fact it blew the lot away
	This glorious hungry army.
Chorus	Sound the bugle, blow the horn . . . *etc.*
Ditch	I've got a medal as you see
	The workhouse gave it out to me
	For hanging fast to a rotten tree
	When the wind took the hungry army.
Chorus	Sound the bugle, blow the horn . . . *etc.*

The lull before the storm. Dusk. The crew lean, loiter as they sing the last chorus. Cuttle plays his whistle, alone, for himself

Hannah There's something about the night air. Brings the thought of home somehow.

Flegg A wise man don't take memories into war.

Hannah Won't be long now, will it. Trumpets. Clouds and smoke and fire. Flags in the wind.

Flegg Oh ay. Blood running in the gunnels. Men sank to the bottom. Men in flames.

Hannah And glory.

Flegg Oh ay. Glory. Who wants a piece of cheese? (*He hands some round. It's from his pocket, hard to carve*)

Ditch There's hairs on it.

Flegg Pick 'em off then. Hairs. There's been times I've been about to eat my boot straps. Hairs.

They eat in silence

Drubber A piece of Suffolk cheese. Come Christmas I'll always have a piece of Suffolk cheese.

Cuttle Think of them, eh, toes poked in a roaring fire.

Hannah I wouldn't be anywhere but where I am now.

Flegg I'd 've liked to be home for Christmas with my old woman.

Cheers and shouts off

Drubber There's the extra rum.

All rise. Cuttle throws Flegg his cheese

Cuttle Here, Fleggie. Save this. Make yourself some buttons.

Flegg Ditch, if I fall you can have my knife.

Ditch I'd sooner have your compass.

Flegg I've promised that my sister.

Ditch What use has she for it?

Flegg It's promised her.

Godbolt enters

Godbolt Go and collect your rum. Grey, stay on watch.

Cuttle (*to Hannah*) I'll get yours, sir.

As they go ...

Ditch That's a good compass, that is. Wasted on a woman.

The others go, leaving Hannah and Godbolt

Godbolt Well, Grey?

Hannah Sergeant?

Godbolt Got the dread in you?

Hannah No, Sergeant.

Godbolt Drum them out of the seas, will you?

Hannah Yes, Sergeant.

Godbolt Yes, Sergeant. They beat us ragged in the last campaign.

Hannah It's different now. We've got the twenty-four pounders now.

Godbolt Some things is never different, Grey. No matter how many campaigns go by. You ask the bastards that's got the long green grass grown over them. You ask them. The bastards that's got fishes swimming in and out of their eyeholes. They say you see things?

Hannah Sometimes, Sergeant.

Godbolt What can you see on the horizon?
Hannah The enemy fleet.
Godbolt And beyond?
Hannah The flash of the sea.
Godbolt And beyond?
Hannah A star. A faint star.
Godbolt And furthest? On the rim?
Hannah Night.
Godbolt That's all.
Hannah Yes, Sergeant.
Godbolt Nothing more?
Hannah Nothing.

A silence

Godbolt It's a dark sea.
Hannah Ay.
Godbolt Every man on this ship, I'm the mother to him and the devil to
   him. I make him steel, I make him seaworthy. But what mother has for
   him ain't meat and tater pie, it's cannon-balls. I can't make him shot-
   proof, Grey. Some nights when the sea's black I think I hear sighs come
   across the waves. All my dead lads. Lines of 'em. All their arms and legs
   and heads, rolling and pitching in our wake. You don't see that?
Hannah No, Sergeant.
Godbolt Nor hear it?
Hannah No, Sergeant.
Godbolt Well, damn you then.
Hannah Sorry, Sergeant.
Godbolt Sorry, Sergeant. Sorry. You're a booby. You're a girl.
Hannah I'm as much a man as any.
Godbolt With your soft eyes and your soft cheeks ...
Hannah Damn all women as bitches. Tow 'em ashore, say I.
Godbolt If you was ... (*He stares at her*) If you was a girl, I'd dance your
   legs out of their britches, I'd plough you into the ground, I'd ... What is it
   about you, Grey? Eh? How d'you draw things out of me, things I'd
   never——

He stares at her, she at him. He hears the others returning

Not a word of this. None of it. Understand? (*As he goes*) Get a beard,
Grey. Get a beard.

   Godbolt exits

   The men enter, drinking

Hannah takes hers, stays on watch away from the rest. Drubber kneels

Drubber O God, O mighty God——
Ditch Here he goes.
Drubber Get me through tomorrow, praise the Lord.
Flegg Stow it, Drubber.

*Drubber mumbles on, a long indecipherable prayer, drinking between. All
drink steadily*

Cuttle Bury me in my best jacket, Ditch.
Ditch You haven't got one.
Drubber (*louder*) May my prayer get up to Thee before my soul——

Ditch kicks him

You blasphemous toad. I'm speaking to my God man to man.
Flegg A quick word should be enough.
Drubber If I die it's your fault, Grey. You boil on God's backside.
Ditch You don't believe all that?
Drubber I'm taking no chances. (*Loud*) Let me not be blown to the bounds
of buggery——
Flegg There's some of us here wants a last bit of peace, and we'll stop at
nothing to get it.

*Drubber subsides into mumbles. Hannah joins them. Flegg cleans his musket,
Ditch and Cuttle wrap themselves in blankets, settle, drink, try to sleep. Cuttle
plays his whistle*

Hannah What's the time?
Flegg Half-way to morning.
Hannah So soon?
Flegg You'll be all right.
Hannah I mean to fight like thunder.
Flegg Oh, ay.
Drubber (*shouting*) O mighty and most powerful Lord, let not a sodding
cannon-ball knock off my head, let——
Flegg D'you want a marlin spike up your arse?
Drubber I'll pray to my poxy Lord whenever I want, you godless fart.
Flegg Another word from your rotting throat——

*As they close in on one another the pipes sound. Instantly they stop. Ditch and
Cuttle rise. All make a chain across the stage passing shot to one another,
filling the tubs*

Hannah Billy, I've a letter here. If anything——
Cuttle Right, sir. Your girl is it, sir?
Hannah My sweetheart's brother. Name of Snell.
Cuttle Oh, that one. The one you're always asking for.
Hannah Ay. That one. (*She fumbles a catch, almost drops a cannon-ball*)
Godbolt (*off*) GREY! You putty-minded dung barge. KEEP IT GOING!
Cuttle I have got one, sir.
Hannah One what?
Cuttle A best coat, sir. Somewheres. For burying.

Godbolt enters

Godbolt (*as he enters*) MAKE SAIL!

The great sail rises, flaps, balloons

Men. We are the Fleet's eyes. We are the Fleet's claws. Ship for ship we've beaten all the navies of the world. Remember what you've learned. Your Frog will fire into the rigging. That's not the British way. Let 'em blast off. We'll wait. That way we'll hear 'em yelp. See 'em fall on their marrow bones for mercy. BLOW 'EM OUT OF THE SEAS!

The crew cheers. Godbolt raises a glass to the ship's company

May we all meet tomorrow.

All cross themselves

Godbolt Three cheers for the enemy. Hip hip——
All HURRAH!
Godbolt Hip hip——
All HURRAH!
Godbolt Hip hip——
All HURRAH!
Godbolt STAND BY YOUR GUNS FORE AND AFT.
All All ready, sir.

Dead silence. All hold their breath

Godbolt Here's a glorious mark. Stand clear. Wait for it. Nice and easy, nice and easy. She's coming at us. Oh, but she's grand. She's coming——

The boom of guns. Bombardment shakes the ship. No-one leaves his place

STAND HARD AS DOGS!

A tremendous splintering crash. The ship rocks. Shrieks off

She's almost on us.

Another bombardment

She's half a cable's length—NOW! FIRE AWAY! HARD AS YOU CAN!

The "Rainbow's" guns open fire. All hell. Darkness, flashes, screams, flags, fire

BLAST HER! BRING DOWN HER MIZZEN!

Drubber is hit, mortally. Hannah tries to help him

Drubber Christ! What have you done to me?

Dazed, Hannah stares

Godbolt (*screaming*) Plug him with his wig.

She does nothing

His wound. Quick. Stuff his wig in it.

She snatches his wig, tries

Drubber You've done for me, you poxy——(*Falling, he grabs at her, her shirt's pulled open, breasts revealed. He tries to speak, dies*)
Godbolt (*screaming*) Keep your bloody thumb in the gun vent. If air gets in the barrel you'll start a fire.

Hannah pulls her shirt close, drags Drubber with her back to the gun. Drubber slides further down, a dead weight. She turns again

What in hell are you gawking at? If he ain't dead call a doctor, if he's a carcass throw him over the rail. He's no good dead.

The battle rises to a crescendo of sound and fury. A huge tearing sound, the sail comes crashing down and envelops Hannah

The crew leave the stage in the turmoil

The Sculleys enter, wrap Hannah in a canvas as though it were a strait jacket

Hannah struggles

Hannah Let me at them——
Mrs Sculley Bless her, she's so easily excited.
Hannah God rot you.
Mrs Sculley Lost to delicacy and refinement.
Hannah See how it shifts and swirls, the battle. How it boils around us, how it screams.

She struggles. They hold her

Mrs Sculley Gently. The doctor says you need no puff and fuss with wrongheads.
Sculley The doctor's only here for half an hour.
Mrs Sculley Well, there's not much money in a maniac. And a physician's time is valuable.
Hannah (*still now*) Wait till you see the whites of their knuckles. Then— (*shouting*) King and country! Glory! Victory!
Mrs Sculley It's a disease, ain't it, Sculley.
Sculley Mrs Sculley, it is. And why we have not caught it's beyond the power of reasoning, but there it is.
Hannah Battle after battle, years of them, on land and sea and sea and land. THE SEA IS OURS BY RIGHT!
Sculley The doctor says more can be done by tenderness than by harshness——

He bangs Hannah briskly on the head with a mallet. She drops limp instantly

But the the doctor don't have the noise and trouble day to day.

The Sculleys exit

Smoke streams across the stage. Hannah lies still on the deck. It is the aftermath of a battle

As the smoke clears, Cuttle crosses to her

Cuttle The surgeon'll be with you soon sir.

Hannah (*whispering*) Billy. Where are we?

Cuttle On the main deck.

Hannah Have we got on a bit. There's that tree.

Cuttle Eh?

Hannah Ain't that the tree that was over there?

Cuttle Er . . . might be.

Hannah (*after a silence*) Well. We made it to tomorrow.

She groans. Cuttle comes closer

I'm not too good, Billy.

He pulls off her coat. It's drenched in blood. So is one leg and thigh

Cuttle Great God Almighty.

Hannah Sh!

Cuttle It's a lot worse.

Hannah SH! We're awful near them. I'd leg it if I was you.

Cuttle You're seeing things. You're safe. You're here on board.

Hannah It's in my groin. Grapeshot.

Cuttle Let go of my hand sir, and I'll——

Hannah I've heard the Frenchies devour women—tear out their hearts and eat them. Have you heard that?

Cuttle I'll fetch the surgeon.

Hannah You feel less windy with a mate. (*A beat*) I think we have.

Cuttle Have what?

Hannah Advanced a bit. (*Her breath rattles*) Hear my breath? Hope they can't hear it. (*A beat*) I'll be better in the morning. (*A beat*) Billy, I can't swallow and there's no cover, nowhere to go, and——(*She sits up suddenly*) It's in my groin.

Cuttle I know.

Hannah We're not in the field, are we. We're aboard.

Cuttle That's right. You're safe.

Hannah Dear God. You'll have to do it.

Cuttle Eh?

Hannah Get your knife.

Cuttle Me? What for?

Hannah You'll have to dig it out.

Cuttle Not me. Not grapeshot in the groin. That's for a doctor.

Hannah I mustn't have the surgeon near me. Not at all.

Cuttle You're off your head, sir.

Hannah Are we mates?

Cuttle Never ask that.

Hannah Do it then. And mind, whatever you see, whatever you find, never a word. Swear.

Cuttle Not a merman, are you, sir?

Hannah On your life and soul. Swear.

Cuttle On my life and soul.

Hannah Good. Clean the blade. And dig.

Cuttle (*hands trembling*) Oh Lord——
Hannah Cut through my britches.
Cuttle Lord oh Lord.
Hannah Must I do it myself?
Cuttle All right. All right. (*He slits the britches*) If that's what you want,
goddammit, sir, I'll have a chop at you. I'll go at you, sir, full tilt, and
then——

A frozen moment. Cuttle stares at the wound, at Hannah, at the wound again

But you're a woman, sir.
Hannah SHH!
Cuttle A woman. And a fine made one at that.
Hannah Am I? Am I, Billy? I've nearly forgot. Well, there. It's told at last.
Been a heavy secret, no-one to trust it to. Now I'm trusting you.
Cuttle A woman aboard's bad luck.
Hannah Remember what you've swore.
Cuttle If they knew——
Hannah If they knew they'd throw me to the sharks. So just you go at it.

Cuttle picks up the knife, holds it shakily, drops it

Cuttle I can't touch you, sir. A woman is uncharted seas to me.
Hannah You can do it. Bollocks man, if I lie here much longer my blood'll
turn to rust.
Cuttle Goddammit, ma'am, I'm doing it, I'm doing it.

Struggling up, she grasps him by the collar

Hannah Cuttle. Call me ma'am again, you'll sink us both. You know what
they'd do to me before they slung me. And they'd flog you, and hang your
bones in chains.
Cuttle Yes, sir.
Hannah It's Jem. Now get to it.
Cuttle Yes SIR. It's a good blade, sir. Gone in very easy, very snug. The
blood's following the knife. It's spreading.

As her gasps grow louder he pulls Davey's kerchief from her pocket

Here, bite on this. Oh bless your heart for a true fellow, sir, here's one.

He holds up a piece of grapeshot. He cuts again. Hannah twists in agony

Hold still. You must hold still.
Hannah (*gasping*) I am.
Cuttle Begging your pardon, sir, you're leaping like a louse. Ah, I'm getting
the hang of it. (*He pulls out another piece*) Here's a deep one here, sir.
Have to make a hole in you. About the size of a crown.

He makes a deeper cut. Hannah cries out. He claps a hand over her mouth

    At that moment Ditch and Flegg appear

With his other hand, Cuttle pulls the coat back over Hannah

Ditch (*wandering over*) What's up with Jem, then?
Cuttle Sprung a leak.
Hannah A scratch.
Flegg You're white as a cod.
Hannah Not ready for the worms yet.
Ditch D'you want a game of rummy?
Hannah I want some sleep, you dogfish. Scram.
Ditch Pox on you, then.

He exits with Flegg

Hannah moans

Cuttle Fought like a gentleman. (*He digs at the shot again*) Here's another bastard. And another. What a thing the body is, eh? A strange mysterious thing. Ah, I'm on the edge of something here, hope it's not your stomach. One more. I'll have to put my finger in, to trace the course of it. Ah. (*He holds up the last piece*) We lose our lives through such a little thing.

Hannah has fainted

Far away, the wind. The beat throbs faintly. The Lights fade down to Hannah

Cuttle exits

Mrs Sculley bustles in, examines Hannah

Mrs Sculley SCULLEY!

Sculley joins her, examines Hannah

Sculley Now what? Still knocked all to pieces.
Mrs Sculley And whose fault's that? She needs reviving.
Sculley He'll be here in half an hour.
Mrs Sculley Well, she's no good to the doctor lying there, is she, like a cod's head in the gutter.
Sculley What d'you think, then? The clay cap? Poultice to the stomach? Cold air to the head with bellows?
Mrs Sculley Water's quickest. Put her in mind of the sea.

Sculley gets a bucket, goes to drench Hannah

No no no. You go at everything so. A small cold stream. Or better, drips and drops.

They drip a little water on to Hannah's head. She comes to

Hannah Tears. On the back of my hand. Oh Davey. Davey. I've called your name in every inn and every church and every jail——
Mrs Sculley You have. She has.
Hannah And now I can't remember you at all.
Mrs Sculley Dear oh dear. You have been in the wars.
Hannah In the wars. Ay.
Sculley Seen the world over.

Hannah Seen it all. You'd think the trees'd cry out, some of the things I've seen. The things I've done.
Mrs Sculley Well, it's a man's life.
Hannah Oh, it's a man's life all right.

The Sculleys exit

The Crew enter

Hannah rises. She has a limp now. She crosses the stage to join the burying party, picking up as she goes a looted hat, which she puts on, and a spade

All the lost lads. The regiment of rattlebones. Well, I don't ride with the dead. You plant 'em, and the tides roll and the grass grows and that's the end of that.

Hannah sings the first verse, Cuttle joins in with his whistle, then the rest gradually until they are all singing

(Singing)   Come and be a soldier, lads, come, lads, come.
                Hark, don't you hear the fife and drum, lads, drum.
                Come to the battlefield, march, march away.
                Come and lose your arms and limbs for thirteen pence a day.

                Come and learn your exercise, lads, run, lads, run.
                Soon you'll know the use of bayonet and gun.
                Then you'll go abroad, my lads, and there you'll soon be warm,
                By shooting men you never knew who never did you harm.

                Now if you should be killed my lads never mind that there,
                You will die with honour, lads, you'll be free of care.
                Don't mind your wives and children for they'll be soon forgotten,
                What's wives and children to you when you're dead and rotten.

All   Oh never be as silly as to fight for kings and queens,
                For none of them is half as good as half a pound of greens.
                Remember what I say, lads, it is a serious thing
                The Almighty made the human race, but never made a king.

A small cove

Hannah, Cuttle, Flegg and Ditch have been detailed to be a burying party. Their work over, they lie at ease. The cove is beautiful, the sun shines. They pass a bottle round. Today the battle went their way. Cuttle wears a looted officer's coat, Ditch a woman's hat and shawl. They have stuck a piece of driftwood in the sand and hung a dead enemy's coat on it. They stone it idly from time to time. Cuttle plays on his whistle

Flegg It'll be another killing day tomorrow. I can smell it.
Hannah I could eat half a ton of turnips.

Flegg (*throwing her an apple*) Here, line your planks with this.

Ditch How do you do it, eh? You've always got your hands on something tasty.

Flegg I look about me, Ditch. There's better things than shawls to plunder.

Ditch rises, rams his hat on Flegg's head and wanders off

Cuttle, you look a proper foul-arsed goose.

Cuttle Eh?

Flegg That coat. You haven't got the stomach for it.

Cuttle I have too.

Flegg It's not frogging and a yard of ribbon makes an officer. It's stomach. Which you have not got.

Cuttle I can chivvy you, and lash you for nothing, as well as any captain, Flegg.

Ditch enters, holding a seashell

Ditch Here, look at this, lads. I'll take this home with me.

Hannah That's a rare one.

Flegg It's a beauty, no mistake.

They pass it round, handle it with delight

Ditch It'll do my son, the rascal.

Cuttle holds it to his ear

Gently, bonehead.

Cuttle I can hear the sea.

Ditch He can hear the sea. Bugger me.

Cuttle Where d'you find it, Ditch?

Ditch points off

Ditch Five to two old Cuttle gets hisself killed.

Cuttle I'm off to find me one.

Cuttle wanders upstage, searching

Ditch Who'll take me. Five to two.

Hannah Was that a drum?

They listen

I hear a drum beat.

Flegg It's in your head, lad. Time enough to hear 'em in the morning.

Hannah I want it to be morning now.

Flegg On fire to get at them?

Hannah Ay. Smack 'em down and pile 'em up.

Ditch Hark at hearty Jem. Looking for a medal?

Cuttle Hey!

Flegg Handful of nettles, that's all medals is.

Ditch You wouldn't say no.

Flegg A medal'd weigh as much with me as a pair of gnat's balls.

Cuttle HEY! Over here.
Ditch He's found the crock of gold.

Cuttle crosses down, pulls at Flegg

Cuttle Hey, Fleggie, come. There's one of our poor lads here, come and see.

Flegg crosses, looks at the bundle Cuttle has discovered. The others follow

Hannah Lord.
Flegg He's finished. Dead of an old campaign.
Hannah Who is he?
Ditch Whoever he is, he's lost the whole works. Ripped from bowel to gullet.
Hannah We should bury him decent, like the others.
Flegg Give us your coat, Cuttle.
Cuttle Why? It's mine.
Flegg We'll wrap his British bones in it.
Cuttle It's not a British coat.
Flegg Are you an Englishman?
Cuttle I hope I am.
Flegg Then off with it, you pox.
Cuttle It's fair spoils and it's mine.
Hannah Billy, get it off.

Cuttle takes it off sadly. They shove the bundle into it, tie the sleeves. They drink

Flegg Poor lad. He'll never hear our anchor splash in British waters.
Hannah Death's a bastard.
Cuttle It is and all.

They drink

   No more mutton stew and dumplings.
Ditch Ay.
Cuttle Ay. Death's a bastard.

They drink

   He stinks though.

They pick the remains

   Ain't that a stench of garlic in his pits?
Hannah Come on, let's get him bedded.
Ditch (*stopping suddenly*) What if he's not a Briton?

The others stop, stare

   What I'm saying is, is he a true Britisher?

They stare

   What I'm saying is, is this here cadaver an English cadaver or is it not?
How do we know?

Cuttle You're right. He's right, sir. What if it's one of theirs?

They drop the remains, stand looking at one another

That's garlic right enough.

Flegg Well, damn his blood.

Cuttle He's got my coat.

Ditch (*pelting stones at the remains*) He should be hanged like a dog.

Cuttle (*joining Ditch*) He's got my coat, the pox.

Hannah He's a man, Billy.

Cuttle No, sir. Not if he's a Frog.

Hannah I'll do it alone, then.

Hannah struggles to shift the remains. They watch. With a sigh Cuttle joins her

Ditch You're not burying some ape in a frilled coat like a Christian.

Hannah I am, Ditch.

Ditch Damned if you are.

Hannah Damned if I'm not, then.

They face one another

Flegg It's heatstroke, lads.

Hannah I'll do it alone. I told you.

Ditch And I told you, we're not sweating over some foreign buggeroo——

Hannah Their bones, our bones, what's the difference. A shilling a day, he'll yell and shake his musket. When the call comes he'll stand up to be shot at. Common as lice, we are. The wind blows, like it always blows, on all of us.

A silence

Flegg Plant him.

Cuttle Bed him here. Easier digging.

They drag the body over, dig

Ditch Flegg's right. You're sunstruck.

Hannah (*lifting her head*) Hear that wind?

They stop, listen

Flegg No.

Cuttle There's nothing, sir.

They dig again. The beat begins

Ditch Damned old devil stinkard. Hurry up.

They dig. Suddenly Hannah drops her shovel

Hannah Not here.

Flegg Hit a bed of rock?

Hannah It's full of dead already.

Ditch Can't be. This piece of ground's not been fought over.

Hannah It's choked with dead.

They pick up the body, stand undecided

Cuttle He's seeing it. Seeing it, ain't you, sir.
Ditch See it quick, then. He's a heavy-arsed dog.

The beat is stronger

Hannah Bury the dead. Bury or burn. But first dig out the buried living.
Flegg Eh?
Cuttle It's only ghosts, sir. We'll all be ghosts.
Hannah Dig out the head, then free the limbs.
Flegg Here, lug him over here.

They move. Hannah follows, digs frantically, stops

Hannah But first examine the soil. For who can tell, turning the soil, what dangers lie in the earth.
Ditch What kind of words is that?
Flegg Holy Lord above. Try over here.

They move

Here, Jem?
Hannah No. It's filled.

They move. The wind begins

Flegg Here?
Hannah No. Too many shadows. White. They're everywhere.

They move

Cuttle Here, sir?
Hannah Oh Christ. The wind. It blows on all of us.

They stare, cross themselves, move on

Cuttle Here, sir? Sir, here?
Hannah No, no, no, no.
Cuttle For Christ's immortal sake, then, where?
Hannah There's nowhere. Nowhere. (*A cry*) NOWHERE!

Darkness. The beat strong. The wind howls

CURTAIN

ACT II

The madhouse

Hannah is in her nightdress. She stands in the same place, the same position as at the end of Act I. The others have gone. The Sculleys watch as Hannah sinks, huddled, silent

Mrs Sculley Seems like she's mad as any. Shame.

Sculley Nothing for it now, I'd say. Knowing the doctor as I do.

Mrs Sculley The swing?

Sculley The swing. (*He goes to the swing, pats it, sends it sailing up*) Spick, span and new, Mrs Sculley. (*He swings it down again*) Once upon a time, in the early stages of ignorance, there weren't no such thing as a swing. Funny to think it now. The doctor being so partial.

Mrs Sculley It's a fearsome thing.

Sculley It's a wonder. (*He dusts the chair with his handkerchief*) It's a remedy. Makes 'em vomit. Makes 'em faint. Unloads the vessels and the arteries.

Mrs Sculley Altered, Mr Sculley?

Sculley Altered.

Mrs Sculley To the good?

Sculley (*testing the straps*) Less bulk in the contents of the brain. Contentment.

Mrs Sculley Not for all. Some only whisper. Some only kneel and stare.

Sculley There's always the element of chance. A comfortable number comes out tip-top.

Mrs Sculley And it's a good sight. (*Out front*) One of the sights of London. And a person has to live.

Sculley (*out front*) Should keep you in good spirits. Talking of which, (*holding out his cap*) I've no objection to a drop of gin myself.

Mrs Sculley Well said, Sculley.

They look out expectantly. Hannah suddenly stands, hands still covering eyes

Hannah Cover your eyes. Don't look into the sky.

Mrs Sculley Off again. No peace for the wicked.

Hannah Heat like light and light like heat——

Sculley Cunning as Old Nick himself.

Hannah I can see the bones in my fingers. Red.

Mrs Sculley Even he don't know half the tricks she's up to.

Hannah My eyes are closed and I can see them. Smoking. (*Holding her hands out to the Sculleys*) Look. They're smoking. Look.

Mrs Sculley (*as they throw her on the bed*) Oh bless you, I'm so fond of her—don't ask me why. Play her some music. Sculley. Soothes a lunatic, the doctor says. Play her a tune, poor thing.

Sculley plays a tune on comb and paper

> *It's taken up by Cuttle on his penny whistle as he enters*

> *The Sculleys exit*

Susan's house

> *Susan comes in, sits by the bed waiting*

She takes the coat off Hannah, covers her with a blanket. Cuttle picks up his coat, folds it, puts it under her head. Susan takes it out, hands it back to Cuttle, replaces it with a pillow. All hushed, careful

Susan Thank you.

Cuttle sits again on the floor

> You can't stay here any more. I'm sorry. You can't expect——
Cuttle I don't expect nothing ma'am. I've found it best.
Susan Good. We've no bed, you see. No sheets.
Cuttle Don't trouble over me, ma'am. I can sleep in a horsepond.
Susan We don't have a horsepond.
Cuttle See, where he goes, I go. I'm his.
Susan Where SHE goes. I'm HERS. Oh dear. I know I sound unkind. I am unkind. But Caleb's laid off and the winter's coming and it's been three months now and you're still here all over my floor and——

Hannah wakes

> How are you, dear?
Hannah I'll do. Dammit, I meant to wake, Susan.

Hannah gets out of bed, dresses in shirt and skirt

Cuttle Polishing the steps, sir, if I'm needed.

> *Cuttle exits*

Susan coughs hard

Hannah Where's the goose fat? I'll rub your chest.
Susan It's for Caleb. His chest's bad.
Hannah So's yours.
Susan It's for him.
Hannah (*kicking the hem of her skirt*) I'd like to have done with bloody skirts forever.
Susan Well you can't. You're ashore.
Hannah Grounded. Don't I know it. All my old comrades gone. They don't want to know me now, like this. (*She kicks her skirt again*)
Susan I've to see to the beer. Why don't you give me a hand.

Hannah stares out moodily

> Hannah? Help me.

Hannah Eh? Why bother. You don't like beer.

Susan Caleb does.

Hannah Oh rot me. Caleb says. Caleb wants. What about you?

Susan It's what he wants that matters.

Hannah Why?

Susan Because men are the ones. It says so in the Bible. That's why they lay on top of us.

Hannah Hanged if I'd let Davey have everything his way if he'd come back. But you don't come back from the bottom of the sea.

Susan stares at her

Susan You know.

Hannah I think I knew it all along. I saw it, didn't I. And what I see . . . How did he die?

Susan In Portugal. About four years ago. His captain came to see us.

Hannah How, though?

Susan Well, he died in a fight. Leave it a bit, love . . .

Hannah Tell me.

Susan You've been so ill . . .

Hannah I'm strong now. Tell me.

Susan In a brawl. How else? He killed a man. Drove a knife through his neck. They caught him. They—I can't say it.

Hannah You must. You have to.

Susan They put a rock in each hand and a big stone round his neck. They tied him in a sack. Then they slung him in the harbour.

Hannah And he sank. His shadow turned under the water . . . and he sank. Poor lad. Poor lad.

Susan (*collecting a note*) He gave me this. The captain. (*She hands it to Hannah*)

Hannah "God prosper you, Han, till I get to heaven which there's no fear of, your Davey." (*A beat*) He's written it good. Spelt "heaven" right and all. (*A beat*)

Susan He was a rat.

Hannah I'd like to have seen him, though.

Susan And so should I.

Hannah All those years I ached for him. Empty arms. Empty belly. I tell you, the next man I see, if he's anything at all, I'll have him.

Susan Hannah!

Hannah Couldn't he make us laugh, though. Seems so long ago. Nobody's called me Han . . . and he killed a man.

Susan It was dirty luck, the captain said, they were both as rough as each other.

Hannah Well, I'm as bad, ain't I. I've killed.

Susan Not like that.

Hannah Just like that.

Susan You fought to save us from our enemies. So we could sleep in peace.

Hannah I fought to save my neck. The first lad I killed, he stood and looked at me, face as white as a wig, holding his stomach in his hands. I took it to be his stomach. I was young then. Could have been his bowels or his lights.

Susan But he was an enemy.

Hannah Rot me, you stupid girl. Our guts is all the same.

A silence

Susan I lit that lamp for you every single night, and when that Mr Cuttle carried you in, so weak, so troubled in your mind, I thought I'll never be happy, never. You were a sister to me, and a friend. But now there's nothing left. Nothing I say is right. You think I'm dull, and Caleb. I know you've been to war and done hard things, exciting things. Well, it's been hard at home. Right now we don't know where the next meal's coming from. How's that for hard?

Hannah I didn't know.

Susan Well, now you do.

Hannah I'll find something in the morning.

Susan What's wrong with now?

Hannah I'm known, you see. They point at me, they gawp.

Susan We're watching all our things go one by one to keep you and that Billy Cuttle in good health. Know what Caleb said? She's your Hannah, he said. Let them both stay as long as they like, he said, we'll manage. He's a fine man for all he's not a bloody soldier, and his chest is bad, and I hope that makes you die of shame.

Susan bursts into tears. Hannah crosses to her, hugs her

Hannah Oh Susie, Susie——

Susan I should have my tongue speared with a fork.

Hannah Why didn't you say before?

Susan How could I? You was sick.

Hannah I'm all right now. You've took good care of me. I'm free. (*She hugs her again, yells*) BILLY! (*She crosses to exit*)

Susan Where are you going? Hannah? (*Rushing after her*) Hannah you're not to be reckless——

Hannah Somewhere I should have gone a month ago. To the Duke of Cumberland.

An ante room

Cumberland is pinning a medal on Godbolt

Cumberland Don't know what you did but whatever it was you did it damn well.

Godbolt exits

Hannah marches in, waits at the entrance

No women. Sorry, no. I'll see no wives today.

Hannah Excuse me, Your Grace——

Cumberland Out with you missie.

Hannah I'm to give you this. (*She hands him a petition*)

Cumberland "... Maketh oath of faith that this deponent Hannah Snell
..." Good God. Remarkable. Heard of you of course. "... served His
Majesty King George ... entered herself as a Marine ..." And here you
are. Well well.

Hannah They told me I should see you.

Cumberland Quite right, quite right. "... wounded at Pondicherry ...
returned without the least discovery of her sex ..." Wounded, eh?

Hannah Twelve times, Your Grace.

Cumberland Well done.

Hannah Three of them serious.

Cumberland Well done well done. Pondicherry eh? Awfully grand battle.

Hannah It's my leg, Your Grace.

Cumberland My God, what I wouldn't give to have been there.

Hannah Some days it's stiff as a sword. They said you'd pension me.

Cumberland Did they?

Hannah They did.

Cumberland Well, here's a predicament.

Hannah A shilling a day, they said.

Cumberland Did they indeed? Alas, can't be done.

Hannah Why not?

Cumberland You're a woman.

Hannah What's that to do with it?

Cumberland Enlisting under false pretences. Lucky you're not in gaol.

Hannah I fought as well as any man. Three sieges, two important expeditions, six pitched battles——

Cumberland Grand, how grand.

Hannah Seven years I gave——

Cumberland And what a privilege.

Hannah I can't get no work. No-one'll have me. There's too much talk
about me.

Cumberland You can hardly be surprised at that. A female, living among a
hundred men. Half naked, most of 'em. (*Eyeing her*) Rolling about at
night on the hot deck.

Hannah I know men have got a ten pound for a wound and I have twelve.

Cumberland Have you indeed. Show me.

Hannah Show you what?

Cumberland Your wounds, girl.

Hannah (*backing a little*) You're drunk.

Cumberland Lovely little thighs. Plump as chickens. (*Catching her arm*) Tell
me your dreams. You gallant girl, whisper your dreams to me. Put me to
bed, you pussy cat.

Hannah (*escaping*) I'll put you to bed all right. With a shovel.

Cumberland God yes. That's it. I attempt to board, you repulse me——

Hannah One move and I'll bite your nose off.

Cumberland So coarse. You glorious creature. Kiss me, goddess.

Hannah Kiss you? Never. You've a face like a dogfish.

A silence. Dangerous. Then Cumberland, genuinely amused, laughs

Cumberland Well done, well done. Fought like an Englishman. Stupendous. I'll make you a present.

Hannah I don't want a present. I want my rights.

Cumberland My dear young friend, you have no rights. I thought I made that clear. I'm sorry for you. But the purse ain't bottomless.

Hannah I'm to get nothing, then.

Cumberland Have you no property? A little annuity, perhaps? A sockful of guineas? A few pounds for expenses? Dear me.

Hannah I'd go back to sea but they won't have me now.

Cumberland I see your dilemma. I do indeed. Damn me if I don't take this and show it to the King.

Hannah Oh, sir——

Cumberland Do what I can.

Hannah I knew you'd help me, sir.

Cumberland (*gathering papers*) Face like a dogfish! Damn lucky I didn't send you to the treadmills. But I like you. Come and see me any time you want. (*As he leaves*) I trust you'll find some means of amusing yourself.

Cumberland exits

Cuttle enters, with Godbolt

Cuttle Well, that'll send him scuttling for his ma. "Bite your nose off", eh?

Hannah Billy, you ain't been——

Cuttle What's keyholes for? Me and Sergeant Godbolt here——

Hannah Hell's teeth. Invite the Fleet why not.

Cuttle He were just leaving as we came.

Hannah In the same boat?

Godbolt Adrift.

Hannah Good to see you, Sergeant.

Godbolt Godbolt. I've no ship now.

Godbolt and Hannah eye one another

So. You're a woman then.

Hannah I am.

Godbolt I heard the talk. Pleased as a pike with yourself, no doubt.

Hannah I did all right.

Godbolt Well, you can keep a secret, I'll say that for you. That Davey Snell you was after——?

Hannah My husband.

Godbolt Where's he then?

Hannah Dead.

Godbolt So you sailed for nothing?

Hannah I'd not have missed it. None of it.

Cuttle Nothing's what we've got from it.

Godbolt The world's against a fighting man, once the war's done.

Cuttle Treat you like a dog. Or worse.

Godbolt I'm nothing without my ship. A hollow man.

Hannah Seems I'm not a proper female. Nor a man neither. You're not the only one adrift.

Cuttle All doors shut to us. And winter coming. It'll be hard.

A short silence

Godbolt There's sleet in the wind.

Cuttle Some god has a bag, don't he, with the four winds in. He's meant to
let them out in turn, but it's only the cold one I ever see. I think God hates
the poor.

A short silence

Godbolt I'm a man needs to be doing.

A short silence

Cuttle Well, three's better than one, that's what they say.

Godbolt Do they?

Cuttle Why don't we stick together?

Godbolt A ramshackle crew. A woman, a waxwork and a hollow man.

Hannah Ladies and gentlemen, by ticket only, one of the sights of London.
The Woman, The Waxwork and the Hollow Man.

They sigh

We've lost our place, that's all. We have to find another.

Cuttle If I don't eat something soon——

Hannah Looks like we'll have to sing for our supper.

A short silence

Cuttle We could, too. Sergeant Godbolt, sir, he could. (*To Hannah*) You
could.

Godbolt Eh?

Cuttle Sing. He could sing. In public.

Hannah No, I——

Cuttle There'd be money in it.

Hannah No, I——

Cuttle He's good.

Hannah But I——

Godbolt Have to be bloody good. Who'd come?

Cuttle All of 'em. Everyone. He's known. Stopped in the street. Drawn
pictures of. The Woman Warrior. The Tantalizing Tar. They'd come all
right.

Hannah To poke at the caged bear. I'm buggered if I'll——

Cuttle Remember how we'd hear him in the dog watch, in the lantern light?
All the men'd go still. We'd forget our bellies, and the rope, and the day
that was to come. You'd sing, sir, and we'd see the hills of home.

Godbolt Let's hear you.

Hannah What, here? Now?

Godbolt Don't muck about.

Hannah What'll I sing?

Cuttle A sea song. Like you used to.

Hannah I was a boy then.

Godbolt Be a boy now.

Hannah strikes an attitude, opens her mouth, closes it again

Hannah You put me off.

Godbolt Never mind me.

Hannah I'm nothing. Ten a penny.

Godbolt Don't simper. It don't suit you. Sing.

Hannah Let me go home and——

Godbolt SING!

Hannah (*immediately, in anger, as a boy, straight at him*)

> Fifty I got for selling my coat,
> Fifty for selling my blanket.
> If ever I list for the army again
> The DEVIL shall be my sergeant.

Godbolt We're getting somewhere.

Hannah I don't feel right.

Godbolt You don't look right. What I hear don't match what I see.

Cuttle You did ought to be a boy again, you suit a shirt and britches.

Godbolt Right. This is how it goes. You've a reputation in the town. We'll use it. You'll sing the songs of war. You'll sing 'em as Jem Grey. You'll wear full regimentals, we'll get a special dispensation off the King.

Cuttle The King? The devil to catch hold of is the King.

Godbolt Not us, booby. We'll use Cumberland. He has the King's ear. (*To Hannah*) You'll go to him. Talk sweet.

Hannah Sooner sit on a hornet's nest.

Godbolt D'you want to eat?

Hannah What'll I say?

Godbolt Tell him you've found a means of amusing yourself.

Hannah Music. What about music?

Cuttle I can play, sir. Anything you can whistle, I can play.

Godbolt Right. You sing. He plays. I drill you.

Hannah Drill?

Godbolt We'll make a thing of it. Your soldierliness. Such as it is. I'll take you through your motions, a different thing each night, that'll keep 'em coming.

Cuttle takes out his whistle, plays the start of a march

For God's sake, man. She'll not be hopping about in the streets while we scramble for coins. We do it proper on a stage or not at all. (*Taking coins from his pocket*) Buy us a fife and drum. These are my savings, understand? Don't throw 'em in the sea. Be back by nightfall or I'll see your backbone.

Hannah It's not your ship. We're not your crew.

Godbolt Think I don't know? Think I can't see where I've fallen to? Primping with a woman and a waxwork on a painted stage. Move, Cuttle.

Cuttle Trust me, sir. I've an eye for a job like this, sir, Sergeant, sir. (*As he goes*) I'll come back with as sweet an instrument as you ever saw.

He exits

Godbolt Must he tag on?
Hannah Billy's my friend.
Godbolt The man's a carbuncle.
Hannah Leave him alone. We're equals now.

They eye one another

Godbolt If anything comes of this, I'm in command.
Hannah On stage.
Godbolt Don't look to me to lark about with you. You've him for larks. Expect no comradeship from me. I know nothing of it.
Hannah You don't get a fig from a bramble.
Godbolt That's understood, then.

They shake hands. A short silence

Women don't belong in war.
Hannah Bollocks.
Godbolt The sights of war ain't fit for 'em.
Hannah I fought the same as you.
Godbolt It's wrong. Got to be. Against God. Against nature.

A short silence

Seven years we beat about the seas together.
Hannah Faced smoke and fire.
Godbolt Heard the ice crack and the water run. Now I'm to call you Hannah.
Hannah It's my name.
Godbolt If I don't care to?
Hannah Call me anything you like. No odds to me.
Godbolt I'll call you nothing.
Hannah Right.
Godbolt Nothing's what we are. Shadows. The forgotten.
Hannah Shadows. Forgotten.
Godbolt After a victory I used to think—today, me and the lads, we done a thing all right. Today we turned back history, wheeled it on its arse. But it rolls by. They don't remember.

Hannah shivers, stares out

Hannah Who will remember us? Who will remember? There'll be nobody left to remember.
Godbolt Eh?
Hannah Only our shadows. White. On rocks. On walls.
Godbolt What the hell's up with you?
Hannah Something I see.
Godbolt See? Thought you'd done with that.

A bumping and clanking off (from Cuttle). Hannah shakes her head clear

Hannah Lord. I did too.
Godbolt Tell you what I see. A muckfly.

Cuttle enters. He is encased in a one-man band—drums, fife, trumpet, cymbals, bells, tambourine, triangle

Cuttle (*breathless*) Here I am, sirs both, and here we are.
Godbolt God Almighty.
Cuttle (*organizing it round him, adding his whistle*) How's this, sirs?
Hannah Amazing.
Godbolt What kind of din comes out of that contraption?
Hannah Can you play it? Can you get a tune?
Cuttle It's a matter, sir, of knowing your way round the bits of string. A ting here and a thump there—there's a sort of a list to starboard, sir, can you give me a haul. The bargain of all time, this, sirs, and some to spare. (*He shuffles over to Godbolt, gives him some coins*)
Hannah Well done, Billy. We can have lights. And scenery. A storm at sea——
Cuttle We'll chill 'em all right, sir. (*He makes sound effects—gulls, waves etc.*)
Hannah The waves toss terrible, the clouds hang black and low——
Cuttle A fog rolls dreadful from the distant shore——
Hannah A lantern for the sun, rising from the fog——
Godbolt WHEN YOU'VE DONE! We'll have no unrehearsed antics. Understand?

Hannah and Cuttle look at him, at each other

Hannah (*singing*)   Fifty I got for selling my coat
                         Fifty for selling my blanket
                         If ever I list for the army again

Cuttle joins in

Hannah
Cuttle } (*together*) The DEVIL shall be my sergeant.

Cuttle drums, marches. Hannah hitches up her skirts, marches

Godbolt HALT! Call yourself a Marine, Snell? Look at the way you stand. The way a Marine stands is like the book of his life. One look and I can read that you know NOTHING! Nothing of God or man or beast or wine or water. NOTHING! CUTTLE!

A wavering trumpet call. Cuttle gets his band going, doing a kind of soft-shoe shuffle as well. A tune lurks somewhere. It ends. A short silence

LAMENTABLE, Cuttle.
Cuttle I don't seem to have no power over it.
Godbolt I've taken a particular hatred to it. You'll get the upper hand of it or you'll be OUT.

Cuttle tries again. Improved

Better, Cuttle. On my stage every man jack has his place. Every man a wheel, a crank, a cog. All moving with a wonderful precision. And under MY command.

Hannah Doing our best, sir.
Godbolt Right. Marching in cadence.

Cuttle drums

The military step of the Romans. It is for this that marches were made. It is for this the drum beats.

Hannah marches

March neat. March regular. A resolute Marine's a formidable sight. Better. Courage and discipline. That's it. March with a bold, imposing air.

Hannah marches off boldly, imposingly. Cuttle follows. They march to the dressing-room

A dressing-room

Hannah changes. Cuttle puts on a regimental hat, helps Hannah into her jacket. Music and a rowdy crowd, off

Godbolt enters

Godbolt Two minutes.
Cuttle Lord. Thought we had at least twenty.
Godbolt We did. There was a conjuring horse which was to have come, but hasn't.
Hannah Godbolt——
Godbolt We follow some simpering loon performing on harmonic glasses. You can only be better.
Hannah Godbolt. I can't go on.
Godbolt Eh?
Cuttle He feels sick.
Godbolt I don't like sickly boys. They piss me off.
Hannah Godbolt. Please——
Godbolt I long to cut off their ears. Remember?
Hannah I remember.
Godbolt You can be sick as a horse in here. But you puke on my stage, I'll kick you over the edge.
Hannah I've heard them out there.
Godbolt It's war. You've been in war, you know how to fight. That's not the enemy out there. No more than the lads on the other side's your enemy in battle. Your only fight's with your own fear. Fear'll lock your bones and close your throat. Fight it. Understand?

He puts a hand on her shoulder. They stand in silence

Got your sea legs?

Hannah nods

They're animals. They're nothing. The backside of the town. Stand your ground. Hurl your songs at 'em like rocks. (*He marches to the side, ready to make his entrance*) You'll be all right. Head up. Chest out. And don't forget to breathe.

On stage

Cuttle provides musical punctuation

Godbolt Ladies and gentlemen. Wonder of Wonders! A bold intrepid Woman, and an English woman, to the honour of her Sex and Country be it spoken, who knew how to keep a Secret! HANNAH SNELL!

Drum roll

Her story is well known. With her natural Intrepidity and Sprightliness she soon became a Tar of Note! Cruelly wounded, she chose almost to Die upon the Spot rather than have the Secret of her Sex revealed! In every way a True and Well-proportioned Woman, as you will see tonight, she has the real Soul of a Man in her Breast. Ladies and Gentlemen— HANNAH SNELL——

Drum roll

THE FEMALE WARRIOR—WILL REPRESENT FOR US——

Fanfare

Hannah marches on

—THE JOVIAL TAR!

Hannah dances the hornpipe, Cuttle accompanying. They bow, fanfare

What Storms she has weathered! How many times has she faced Death! Now, here, tonight, safe in Port at last, HANNAH SNELL, known to her fellow Tars as James Grey——

Drum roll

—dressed in her Regimentals from Top to Toe with all the Accoutrements requisite, will go through the whole Catechism of her Military Exercises. Ladies and gentlemen—HANNAH SNELL!

Fanfare

THE DISCIPLINED MARINE!

Cuttle plays everything, full blast, Hannah drills. Cuttle drums, one, two, timed to fit with Hannah's movements. The drill is graceful, rather than the angular precision of today, more of a flowing whole

To prime and load, twenty-one motions
Join your right hand to your firelock.
Recover your firelock
Pose. Open your pan.
Handle your cartridge.
Open your cartridge.
Prime.

Shut the pan.
Load with cartridge.
Draw your rammer.
Shutter your rammer.
Ram down your cartridge.
Withdraw your rammer.
Return your rammer.
Shoulder.
As the front rank, make ready.
Present.
FIRE!

Godbolt then takes Hannah through her sword drill. Flashy, lots of swank and wide sweeps and arcs. Cuttle's drumming is correspondingly ornate

What Marine, how wellsoever disciplined, ever exercised his Small Arms better on the Poop and Quarter Deck? Who fired his Pontoon, who brandished his Sword with more Bravado? HANNAH SNELL is the just Object of universal Admiration. A small poem, written by myself, in honour of this matchless Amazon . . .

> 'Twas thought Achilles' greatest glory
> That Homer rose to sing his story.
> But Hannah's praise no Homer needs
> She lives to sing her own great deeds.

Tremendous fanfare from Cuttle. Hannah sings

Hannah   All ye noble British spirits
              That midst dangers glory sought
              Let it lessen not your merit
              That a WOMAN bravely fought.

              Cupid slyly first enrolled me
              Pallas next her force did bring
              Pressed my heart to venture boldly
              For my love and for my king.

              In the midst of blood and slaughter
              Bravely fighting for my king
              Facing death from every quarter
              Fame and glory there to bring.

              Sure you'll own 'tis more than common
              And the world proclaims it so
              Never yet did any WOMAN
              More for love or glory do.

They bow and leave the stage

The dressing-room

Cuttle is putting the finishing touches to Hannah in her regimentals

Cuttle Out there again, sir.

Hannah Who?

Cuttle Old welldonedamnwelldonegodyes. Him.

Hannah Good. He's back.

Cuttle He's always back, ain't he.

Hannah Well, let him in.

Cuttle Sniffs after you like a dog in a boneyard.

Hannah Billy, let him in.

Cuttle You did ought to rest up. After that bit of trouble last night. You don't look right to me.

Hannah Don't fuss.

Cuttle I'm not fussing. I'm saying. And another thing I'm saying is a long nose and a frilled shirt don't make you God Almighty.

Hannah Do I do it myself?

Cuttle grumbles off, returns with Cumberland

Cumberland Aha. My little female gladiator.

Cuttle He's on in five minutes.

Cumberland You look superb.

Cuttle (*under his breath*) Godyesdamnyes.

Hannah Thank you, Billy.

Cuttle leaves darkly

How was Prussia?

Cumberland Corrupt. (*Arranging her sash*) Damn you look grand.

Hannah I do don't I?

Cumberland Money, always money, nothing but money, that's your Prussian for you. Whether a minister or his secretary, they're all rapacious. Speaking of money, though . . . (*He holds out a thick official envelope*)

Hannah You've done it!

Cumberland His Majesty is graciously pleased that——

Hannah Cumberland! (*She rushes to him, whirls him round*)

Cumberland He's here tonight.

Hannah (*a moment of apprehension*) The King? Out there?

Cumberland He'll make a presentation. After your act. A shilling a day.

Throwing apprehension away, Hannah hugs him again

Eighteen pounds, five shillings a year, for the term of your natural life.

Hannah How did you do it?

Cumberland Told him you'd personally polished off fifty Frenchies. (*He organizes her epaulettes*)

Hannah Great God. Fifty?

Cumberland His Majesty's passionately fond of French Literature. But he can't abide a Frog.

Cuttle races in

Cuttle We've a full house. (*He reties her sash*) Don't be afraid, sir. You'll be all right.

Cumberland Miss Snell's afraid of nothing, Cuttle.
Cuttle (*adjusting her epaulettes*) I'm there with you sir. Remember that.

Cuttle dashes out

Hannah stands ready

Cumberland I'll be there too. Out front.
Hannah You've seen it seven times already.
Cumberland Eight. And not for a month. I never tire of it.
Hannah You soon will. They all will.
Cumberland My dear, the town is dazzled by you.
Hannah The town hopes I'm a freak. A man with breasts or a girl with bollocks, that's what the town hopes for.
Cumberland God I adore you when you're coarse.

Godbolt enters

Godbolt Steady? Nothing on your mind?
Hannah Nothing.
Godbolt Don't want no trouble. Not tonight. Right. Half a minute, then.

He exits

Cumberland Trouble?
Hannah It's come back again.
Cumberland Damn wounds playing up?
Hannah I wish the King weren't in tonight.
Cumberland The King knows your worth. In the common mind you've come to stand for something grand. The spirit of the Empire. Hannah, little Hannah, you shine on that stage like a jewel.

Cumberland exits

Fanfare (from Cuttle). She moves toward the stage, turns

Hannah You don't understand.

Another fanfare. She puts her hands over her ears

When it comes I can't stop it.

A great drum roll

She turns back, marches out and on to the stage

On stage

Godbolt In this dastardly age of the world, when effeminancy and debauchery have taken the place of love and glory, see before you a woman who has raised herself to the summit of heroism and renown. The remarkable—HANNAH SNELL!

Flags, lights, music

Hannah   All ye noble British spirits
                   That midst dangers glory sought

> Let it lessen not your merit
> That a woman bravely fought . . .

She falters, the beat begins

> . . . In the midst of blood and slaughter . . .

> . . . Blood and slaughter . . . blood . . .
> In the midst of blood and slaughter
> Bravely fighting for my king
> Facing death from every quarter——

> . . . There's blood in the wind. A sea of it. Hear it? We drown
> in it.

Cuttle (*hissed*) Bear up, sir. Please sir.
Hannah (*looking desperately at Cuttle*) It's back.
  (*Singing*)   Sure you'll own, 'tis more than common
> And the world proclaims it so
> Never yet did any woman——

She stops. Cuttle's music trails off. A silence

(*Speaking*) More for love and glory do. Oh, it's a glorious life all right. Men flapping round the battlefield like crows at dusk. Shrieking after their lost limbs. Men's hands and arms and legs enough to make a hill, men's blood to fill a ditch. (*She slashes at the flags with her sword, rips them through*) God rot all swords and flags. (*She hurls her sword away*) God rot glory!
Godbolt Marching in cadence. The military step of the Romans——

Cuttle rolls his drum

Hannah (*shouting above them*) Come and lose your eyes and limbs for twelve fine pence a day——
Cuttle Please sir. The King.
Godbolt (*hissing*) March. For Christ's sake, march.
Hannah The King. God save the King. (*Shouting, not singing*) Oh never be as silly as to fight for kings and queens——

Cuttle moves towards her

For none of them is half as good as half a pound of greens——

Godbolt moves in

Remember what I say, lads, it is a serious thing——
Godbolt (*hissing*) Play, Cuttle. Loud. Loud.
Hannah (*yelling louder*) The Almighty made the human race but——
Godbolt (*grasping her pulling her off with him*) Play, damn you.
Hannah (*yelling*) Never made a king. Glory? It don't amount to a horse's fart.

They lurch off in disarray

Boos from the crowd. A drum beats steadily. The wind blows

The dressing-room

Godbolt pushes Hannah into a chair

   Cuttle enters, disentangles himself from his band

Hannah gasps for breath. Cuttle goes to her

Godbolt Stand aside. Give her air.

Hannah struggles for breath. Godbolt slaps her face a couple of times, not hard. She comes to

   Head between your knees. Up. Breathe steady. Good.

   Cumberland strides in

Cumberland Is her mind cleared enough to talk to me?
Godbolt She'll do.
Cumberland She looks white.
Cuttle Takes a while now for the sights to leave him.
Cumberland This has happened before? Here? In this theatre? Before everyone?
Cuttle Never as bad as this.
Cumberland How often?

Cuttle doesn't want to answer

   How often?
Cuttle Three times.
Cumberland Damn. What's she said?
Godbolt Senseless. Shadows. Danger from the sky, rain that eats forests, dead seas. Babble.
Cuttle And the wind, always the wind.
Godbolt Never the King, your grace. Never the regiment.
Cumberland Treason. Treason, dammit.
Cuttle Anyone as thinks Jem Grey a traitor——
Cumberland Is she a lunatic?
Hannah Bollocks no I'm not.
Cumberland Better for you if you were. Dammit, it won't do. To see you take your sword and rip the splendid fabric of the Empire——
Hannah When it comes I can't do nothing.
Cumberland I'm afraid you must. The King's displeased. He's anti-français. We may at any moment see a rekindling of the wars. You raise questions that may not be raised. (*He starts to go, turns*) It's injudicious, mischievous and ill-advised. (*He crosses to Hannah, touches her cheek briefly*) Chilled. Damn. (*He leaves, at the last moment he turns again*) Your pension's sunk for good. And try this one more time, you'll find yourself in Bedlam. It won't do, d'you see. I merely pass on what I'm asked to pass on.

He goes

A short silence

Cuttle You've done it now sir.

Godbolt Trust a bloody woman.

Cuttle We was doing so grand, too. The pension too, and all. We'd have been snug as weevils in a biscuit tub.

Hannah, undressing, folds her regimentals

Hannah Shan't need these.

Godbolt Damn right you shan't.

She places her hat on top, then the sword

Hannah I couldn't stop them, Godbolt.

Godbolt Them?

Hannah The dead. Crowding. Pressing. Their eyes smoking.

Godbolt Thought you loved your duty. And your King.

Hannah They made me speak.

Godbolt Where's your soldier's honour? Where's your pride? (*Holding up a torn flag*) How do we get with honour out of this? You should love the flag like you love your life. Spill blood to save it.

Hannah I couldn't kill again to save the world.

Godbolt Courage run out, is that it?

Cuttle You could search the bible through from end to end and never find a truer, braver——

Godbolt Any man can lose his courage any time. It'll slip through your hands like a rat to the river. Is that it?

Hannah I want no more of war. I see it. Out there. Beyond the rim of the world. How it will be. Terror. Tumult. Desolation. A wind that lays the bedrock bare.

Godbolt If there's any sense to what you say I'm stone blind to it. So's greater men than us.

Cuttle Bedlam. Lord.

Godbolt You've drawn heavy fire.

Hannah Piss off then.

Godbolt (*collecting his things*) I felt shame tonight.

Hannah Christ, do you think I want it?

Godbolt collects Hannah's uniform, sword, hat

Godbolt I made you, steeled you, kept you in best order. For all you're a woman, I thought you was my man.

Hannah Better get yourself another curiosity. A mermaid, or a dog that plays the spoons.

Godbolt (*as he goes*) I hate to feel ashamed.

Godbolt goes

A silence

Hannah You can piss off too.

Cuttle Not me, sir. I stop here.

Hannah I'd sooner march alone.

Cuttle I'm with you, you know that. Any ways. All ways.

A short silence

Hannah Seems I'm a rotten bargain.

Cuttle Without you, sir. I'm nothing. Bone to bone——

Hannah Shadow to shadow.

Cuttle Now sir. Don't go off again.

A silence

Hannah Be strange without him.

Cuttle Better the two of us.

Hannah Him and me ... I thought ...

Cuttle The last of the great sea monsters, that's him. You and me, we're all right as we are.

Hannah That's right.

Cuttle No hectoring. No hollering. "You grub. You tapeworm."

Hannah "I'll crack your nuts for you."

Cuttle "Sail around the Horn before I count to one—ONE! Too slow. Come on Cuttle, you——"

Godbolt enters, stands

Godbolt WHEN YOU'RE DONE!

They freeze

     This is what we do——

Cuttle Sergeant, sir, I thought——

Godbolt You thought. I'm the one paid to use my head. You thought she'd sunk us with her sights and visions. Right, Cuttle?

Cuttle Right, Godbolt.

Godbolt Wrong.

Hannah They'll never let me on a stage——

Godbolt Wrong again. You'd be good and fouled without me, both of you. You're notorious. We'll use your notoriety, turn it on its head. But we'll come at it from another tack. Steer clear of drums and swords and flags. See visions, do you? Right, we'll give 'em visions. Stun 'em.

He thumps Cuttle on the back. Cuttle splutters, Godbolt conjures a coin out of his mouth. Cuttle gapes

     Mystery, Cuttle. Magic. Old dogs, new tricks. Right, Snell?

Hannah Right, Godbolt.

Godbolt Right.

On stage

Flashing of lights. Cuttle plays strange oriental music. Godbolt stands in a spot, wearing a black cloak. (The act is a trick, not real to Hannah as the visions are)

Godbolt Ladies and gentlemen, after six months of phenomenal success across the land in the strange and mystic art of mind reading, tonight, for you and you alone, the celebrated HANNAH SNELL.

A spot on Hannah, who now wears a dazzling cloak covered with symbols, moons, stars. She bows. Godbolt holds up a coin

Can any lady or gentleman here tonight distinguish the date upon this coin? (*He holds up an open book*) The page on this? However great the number, writ however small, Hannah Snell can, and shall. For she, with all the other gifts showered upon her by the doting gods, is also DOUBLE SIGHTED.

Hannah stares straight ahead, immobile. Godbolt draws a circle in chalk around her

She will remain here, fixed precisely half-way between Heaven and the Hereafter.

Godbolt goes down among the audience, asks a member near the front

Sir/Madam, d'you have a coin?

A coin is produced

Have I had access to that coin you hold?

The audience member replies

Remember the date. (*He takes the coin, holds it to his forehead*) Look directly at me. Imagine the date. Imagine harder. Harder. Good. (*He hands it back, transmits the information to Hannah*) A moment please for the vibrations to travel across the void. (*To Hannah*) You have received them?

Hannah I have.

Godbolt Tell us the date.

Hannah gives it correctly

(*To the audience member*) Call out your date please.

The audience member does, it's the same

A gift not given to ordinary mortals.

Godbolt moves on, offers a book to another

Hold this book in your left hand. The left. The sinister side. Choose any page you please. Give it into my left hand. Thank you. We are now in direct contact with the hereafter. You can feel it? Concentrate upon your chosen page. Concentrate. (*To Hannah*) Has the edge of the veil lifted?

Hannah It has.

Godbolt Tell us the page number.

Hannah does

(*To the audience*) Is that correct?

It is. Godbolt moves on, offers a pack of cards to another

Do you sir/madam and I know one another? Examine them. Pick one. Place your chosen card against your forehead. (*He takes it after a moment, holds it against his own brow, transmits it to Hannah*) The secret flows from mind to mind. (*To Hannah*) Tell us.

Hannah does

(*To the audience member*) Will you tell us please.

The audience member does, it's the same. Godbolt picks someone with a watch

May we learn the time our friend here has on his/her timepiece. Set it to any time you choose. (*He takes it, holds it up*) Hannah Snell, standing fixed within the magic circle, will tell the hour, the minute. (*To Hannah*) Time?

Hannah gives the correct time

(*To the audience member*) Is that correct?

The audience member agrees. The wind begins to blow. Hannah interrupts

Hannah No. It is not correct. The time is four minutes to midnight. Hear it ticking. Four minutes left for us to say goodbye, before the lights of home go out for good. Before the clock of time stops.
Godbolt Ladies and gentlemen, Hannah Snell, a mind reader who has bamboozled kings and scientists——
Hannah The hands of the clock tick on. Hands ... Our hands ... Our fingers smoke ... Numbers. Great and small, travelling across the void. The void ... Ten ... Ten times brighter than the sun. Ten nine eight seven six five four three two one, once fired it cannot be recalled.
Godbolt (*racing on stage*) I ask for your indulgence. The strain of this mysterious art can sometimes——
Hannah Dates, where are the dates? No dates. No history. The veil will never lift. A pillar of cloud. Bigger than—greater than—darker than——

The wind blows hard, dies down

The Sculleys enter one each side, grab her, silence her

Godbolt and the Sculleys fight for the audience's attention. Cuttle plays desperately

Sculley Ladies and gentlemen——
Godbolt Ladies and gentlemen——
Mrs Sculley (*taking off Hannah's cloak*) You're in luck. The governors is trying to make this by ticket only.
Sculley (*bundling the coat up*) Lose the Londoner his merriment.
Godbolt Hannah Snell is endowed with an extra sense——
Sculley No sense, you mean. (*He throws the cloak off stage*)
Mrs Sculley From the highest to the lowest, man is fond of sights. And lunatics.

Godbolt She'll soon be herself again.
Sculley And as for both together——

The Sculleys try to drag Hannah out of her circle

Hannah The formula of the lethal area. The number of living within the circle will equal the dead without.
Sculley (*shouting above her*) As much liquor as you can drink——
Mrs Sculley (*shouting above her*) And a front seat at a commitment.

Cumberland enters

Complete silence. As he reads the commitment Godbolt and Cuttle freeze

Hannah Cumberland! HELP ME!
Cumberland "I, William Augustus, Duke of Cumberland, do hereby certify that I have seen Hannah Snell of Wapping in the City of London, that she is disordered in her intellects, that she is proper to be, and that I have advised her to be, sent to some house licensed for the reception of lunatics."
Hannah No. Cumberland, NO!
Cumberland Witness my hand and seal this twenty-first day of July one thousand seven hundred and fifty-four.
Hannah Oh, Cumberland.
Cumberland Wretched business. Dammit, I adored you.

He exits

Godbolt and Cuttle melt away

The Sculleys force Hannah into the night-dress she wore at the start of the play

Mrs Sculley (*dressing Hannah*) He's tried, Doctor Kemp. Oh, he has tried. (*To Hannah*) Hasn't he, dearie? Bark, the doctor's tried. And steel. Pills, powders, lotions, potions. Deluged with teas and broths. All as much use as a fistful of rusty nails.
Sculley If you won't allow his curing you today, it's the other place. For life.
Mrs Sculley We need not tell you what that signifies.
Sculley Watch it. Here he comes.
Mrs Sculley Doctor Kemp, God bless him. Now we'll see.

Kemp enters

The Sculleys bow

Sculleys Good-day, Doctor.

They lead Hannah to him. Kemp addresses the audience. Hannah stares ahead

Kemp Case number twenty-eight. A maniacal female, Hannah Snell. Victim of hallucination, an idea which grows and swells and overwhelms the brain. Hannah believes the world lost beyond redemption. Since, through her famous and peculiar history, she is of a somewhat military state of mind, we may awaken her by Sculley beating time.

Ornate drum rolls from Sculley. Hannah stares ahead

Vary the beat, please

A quick march. She stares ahead

Again

Drill rhythm. Hannah snaps to attention

Hannah To prime and load. Twenty-one motions. Join your right hand to your firelock. Pose.

As Hannah continues the drill quietly, Kemp speaks over

Kemp Note the sense of hearing and the sense of sight retain a daily ritual long after that ritual has no further use. Hence the memory of tunes, of——

Hannah, who has now reached the order "Prime", stops suddenly, stands to attention again, speaks strongly

Hannah Survival. Touch nothing.
Cover your hands and feet in sacking.
Cover your eyes in black, your skin in black.
Make a total covering for your body.
Tie it tightly round. Never remove it.
Wear a mask under your hood. Make sure it reaches your Adam's apple.
Never remove it.
Do not sit.
Do not lie down.
Do not eat.
Do not drink.
Never stop trying to protect yourself.

She stands to attention again

Kemp Always her mind returns to her delusions, as the needle to the pole. Hannah, you must let us help you. Why do you think you're here?
Hannah Because I say things no-one wants to hear.
Kemp Why do they not want to hear?
Hannah The things are terrible.
Kemp Why say them, then?
Hannah I must.
Kemp Who says you must?
Hannah The bones. They come into my mind. They say "tell about me".
Kemp What do they say?
Hannah They whisper. A tower of skulls—"we tried hard not to look into the sky". A hill of ribs—"once fired it could not be recalled". A small breastbone—"remember me". A pile of paper flakes—"these were my hands".
Kemp Common symptoms. Fancied whisperings and distant voices. In mania the auditory nerve is in a morbid state, caused by the proximity of the carotid arteries and too much blood to the head. (*To Hannah*) And the

shadows. The white shadows you have told me of. Do these shadows make you speak out against your country?

Hannah Only against war.

Kemp War is a sad and necessary evil. It prevents a greater evil. Cleans the world of wickedness.

Hannah Does it? Ask history. "The King needs the seas". The King's a wolf, he stands at the edge of the woods and howls for meat. To hell with him.

Kemp Enough! Remember, it is not her head, it is her heart which is defective. What are we to do? She has been bled, purged, blistered, drugged, all to no avail. Only the swing remains.

Hannah NO!

Kemp signals to the Sculleys, who drag Hannah, struggling, yelling, across to the swing and strap her in. As they do so—

Kemp It is both a moral and a medical means in the treatment of lunatics. It regulates and diminishes the action of the heart and arteries. Breathing?

Mrs Sculley Twenty in sixty seconds.

Kemp Pulse?

Mrs Sculley Eighty.

Kemp Soon you shall speak of things as they are.

Hannah I say what they are and what they will be.

Kemp Stubborn. Stubborn. Swing.

Sculley sets the swing in motion. The base is in darkness, the high end in bright light. As it cracks up and down Hannah cries out, screams, sobs. Kemp signals for it to stop. Hannah, crumpled, moans, clutches her stomach

Note how the swing calls off the mind from its hallucinations and concentrates attention on the stomach. I find the maddest may be cured. You can see me, Hannah?

Hannah (*it is an effort for her to speak*) Yes.

Kemp Hear me?

Hannah Yes.

Kemp And Mrs Sculley? You can see her?

Hannah nods

This rope? This bowl of water?

Hannah Yes.

Kemp Describe the water.

Hannah The flash of the—a sea, a sea of wind ... Drowned shadows, and beyond ...

Kemp Swing.

Sculley starts the swing up again. Hannah gasps. As it flies up, she speaks, as it crashes down into darkness she cries out. It is fierce and fast

Hannah (*swing up*) And beyond——(*Down, Up*) Heat like light——(*Down, Up*) Last thing alive the fire——(*Down, Up*) Beyond, dead sea, dead moon——(*Down, Up*) On the rim, nothing. (*Down, Up*) No history. (*Down, Up*) No moments. Nothing. And the stars fall.

The swing is stopped. Silence, apart from Hannah's rasping breath. The Sculleys go to her

Mrs Sculley Inspiration fifteen. Pulse sixty.
Kemp Ah. Improvement.

Hannah, freed, stands a moment. Then, blind with dizziness, falls

A degree of vertigo often corrects the morbid state of the intellect.

Hannah retches

There is an intimate connection between the bowels and the intellect. Empty the bowels and you alter the mind. Empty the stomach, the soul is instantly relieved.

Hannah stumbles. Kemp steadies her, strokes her forehead gently

It cannot be too often stressed, never forget tenderness. Your dreams torment you, Hannah.
Hannah Not ... dreams ... awake.
Kemp They will finally destroy you.
Hannah Earth ... destroyed.
Kemp The end of the world is a frequent fantasy among maniacs. (*To Hannah*) The earth will spin long after you and I have gone. Have you no confidence in the mercy and power of God?
Hannah Power ... in ... our hands.
Kemp (*to the audience*) We must break the force of vicious habits. (*To the Sculleys*) Again.

The Sculleys haul a frantic Hannah towards the swing

Hannah No—no—no—no—no——
Kemp One moment.

They stop

Hannah. I know you are capable of reason. You stand at a crossroads. You may save yourself. Give up these bloodthirsty delusions, or be locked away for life.

The Sculleys whisper to her

Sculley To have to go there. Dear oh dear.
Mrs Sculley Some of 'em, to see 'em you'd scream.
Sculley Some's only fit for a cage.
Mrs Sculley Stare you in the face and piss on you. Keep your ravings to yourself. I would.
Kemp Make no mistake. This is your last chance. Do you understand?

Hannah nods

Be careful how you answer. Do bones whisper?

Hannah No.

Kemp What colour is a shadow?

Hannah Black.

Kemp Are there white shadows?

Hannah No.

Kemp What is the strongest weapon that we have?

Hannah The twenty-four pounder.

Kemp Can one single ball kill a man?

Hannah Yes.

Kemp Twenty men?

Hannah Yes.

Kemp Can one destroy a city?

Hannah No.

Kemp Our strongest weapon, the achievement of our finest scientific and
military minds, and it will not destroy a city?

Hannah No.

Kemp Yet you spoke earlier of a weapon that will blast five hundred cities
to the sky.

Hannah Yes.

Kemp A weapon that will blow the trade winds backwards.

Hannah Yes.

Kemp Can the human brain invent anything more fantastical?

Hannah No.

Kemp As fantastical as shadows that are white?

Hannah No.

Kemp As bones that speak?

Hannah No.

Kemp Good. Tell the world. We all wish to hear. I was asleep. Or dreaming.
Or in madness. I did not truly see, and never have.

Hannah I did not—I—I did not ...

Kemp Come, Hannah. Do not disappoint me, please.

Hannah (*low*) I did not see anything.

Kemp And never have. Speak up.

Hannah And never have.

Kemp All's well with God's world.

Hannah All's well with God's world.

Kemp Good, Hannah. You have denied your delusions. Splendid. We are
now on the way to a cure. I shall return tomorrow and ask you the same
questions, and you shall answer in the same way, and so together, gently,
we shall advance to your perfect recovery.

Kemp collects his papers, bows, leaves

Hannah No. NO. KEMP! NO!

Kemp returns

I'm not asleep. I'm not mad. And it's not a dream. Swing me, lock me up,
keep me in the dark. But what I see, I see.

Kemp How sad. To come to this. A nuisance to yourself and to society. Chain her, Sculley. Leave her till dawn, and then, if there's no change, remove her.

He exits

Mrs Sculley Call him back, dearie.
Hannah I can't.
Mrs Sculley Go on. Never too late.
Hannah I can't.

Mrs Sculley puts her arms round Hannah

Mrs Sculley I've got so fond of you.
Hannah Oh, Mrs Sculley.
Mrs Sculley Bless you, I'll come and feed you myself sometimes, for the pleasure of it.

Sculley chains Hannah to the swing

Sculley Nothing personal. A man must make his living.
Mrs Sculley Look. Her eyes is full of tears.

The Sculleys exit

The stage darkens. Hannah sings the last verse of "The Hungry Army". Time has passed

Cuttle creeps in

They hold one another as best they can. They whisper

Hannah Billy. Oh Billy. It's so good to see you.
Cuttle Oh sir. You're altered.
Hannah Been knocked about a bit. How did you get in?
Cuttle Gave a man a coin.

A silence. Cuttle rocks her

Hannah Look after Susan for me, Billy.
Cuttle She don't think much of me.
Hannah Tell her she's not to worry. Tell her——

A noise off

Is that them? That them coming for me?

They listen. No-one

Christ, my heart's drumming. They'll hear it down the passage, make straight for it. (*She shivers*) Must be steady when they come.

Cuttle holds her again

Did Godbolt ...?
Cuttle Never a word.

Hannah He hates what I say. But I thought maybe . . . (*A beat*) Susan, Billy.
  Do the best you can.
Cuttle I will.
Hannah First light of the sun they'll have me in there——
Cuttle Oh sir.
Hannah And they'll chain me down.
Cuttle Oh sir.
Hannah Stood up to 'em didn't I.
Cuttle You did.
Hannah Gave 'em a fight.
Cuttle You did, you did.
Hannah They say they eat their suppers with their mouths. Like dogs.
Cuttle Don't sir. Don't think.
Hannah Sometimes they eat their own flesh. If I'm not mad now I soon will
  be.
Cuttle I'd give all I have to get you free.

A noise off. They freeze

Hannah That's them. It can't be, the moon's still up. Oh God, oh Lord, it's
  them.

Cuttle stands in front of her

Cuttle I'll kill 'em before they have you. By God I will.

Hannah tries to stand

  Godbolt enters

Godbolt Right. What's happening? Why ain't you sawing through that
  chain, garrotting guards, making a rope of sheets?
Cuttle I didn't know—I thought——
Hannah Godbolt——!
Godbolt How many times? It's your duty not to think. I'm the one paid to
  use my head. No need for fancy tricks, I've these. (*Keys*) On watch.

Cuttle stands dazed

  Go on. I'll call you when I'm through.

  Cuttle exits

Hannah I never thought I'd see you.
Godbolt (*unlocking her*) You were wrong, then.
Hannah Oh Godbolt, I'm so glad. Oh, you don't know how good it is . . .
  Oh Godbolt——
Godbolt Keep your voice down. Listen hard. I've been with Cumberland.
  Spoke with him. He don't like to think of you in there no more than us.
  On account of his high place he can't do nothing open, but he's willing to
  wink an eye. But this is it. You must swear an oath, he said. Never to
  speak against the wars again. Nor any other treason.
Hannah He knows I can't. How can I?

Godbolt It's that or Bedlam. Or you live abroad.

Hannah Leave England?

Godbolt Never to beach again on English shores.

Hannah That's cruel.

Godbolt That's how it is. There's a boat. It's yours. Cuttle and I'll get you to it. You have to make your choice.

Hannah England's my home.

Godbolt Tell 'em what they want—you've done with it.

Hannah No.

Godbolt It's a hard thing to stand alone. (*A beat*) Finish with it. Stay. Then we'll go anywhere. Do anything. Side by side. What d'you say?

Hannah It's too late.

Godbolt All for that sheep-brained tosh. Some cannon-ball headed our way that'll drive the earth out of its orbit round the sun?

Hannah Ay.

Godbolt You're yelling into empty air.

Hannah I must. One day there'll be nothing. Not even memory. Not even moments.

Godbolt Eh?

Hannah Moments. What our lives are. A chain of moments. When you smell the morning. When you hear the drum. When you run a rope up like a road and down again like lightning. When a baby's hand closes on your finger. When the breeze blows the blossom, when the wind ... When the horse bends his head to the furrow, when the old man stoops to let the child hear his watch tick. Ten ... nine ... eight ... when the woman remembers the dance. When our children turn at the corner and look back. If we lose these—if we let them go—who will forgive us? There'll be nobody left to forgive us. Understand?

A beat

Godbolt Not a bloody word. You'll sail, then?

Hannah I will.

Godbolt Ain't you afraid?

Hannah Three things you can never say at sea. I can't. I won't ... Come with me.

Godbolt Eh?

Hannah Hear the ice crack——

Godbolt And the water run.

Hannah Will you?

Godbolt You draw me like the tide.

Hannah Then come.

Godbolt Too late. My heart's gone, girl. My soul. Don't know where I lost it, never saw it go.

Hannah Maybe the wars have took it.

Godbolt Maybe they have. Maybe I've stood in blood too long. Smelt the corn in flames too many times.

Hannah Roll up, roll up for the grand life.

Godbolt It's the life I know. King and country, they mean all to me.

Hannah Leave 'em behind, like they've left you.

Godbolt I believe no honour, and no profit, and no safety can come to those who fight against God and the King.

Hannah I believe no honour, and no profit, and no safety can come if I am silent.

Godbolt Well. There it is.

Hannah Ay.

Godbolt You march alone. And so do I.

They stare at one another a moment. Then Godbolt crosses up, hisses

Cuttle! (*To Hannah*) Have to be quick.

Hannah That damn moon's rolling through the sky so fast.

Godbolt Cuttle!

Cuttle enters

Hannah takes off her night-dress (She's dressed underneath still)

We're off and out of here. Swim down river to the boat. No time for explanations. Jump to it.

Cuttle Ay ay, sir.

Hannah (*holding a hand out to each*) For the last time.

The three of them stand linked a moment, then turn. A lighting effect of water fills the stage. They dive and swim through. Gradually the lighting changes, the water becomes sea and sky

The quayside

A small sailing boat. Hannah and Cuttle are in it. Godbolt stands on the quay

Godbolt The water's whipping.

Cuttle Where do we go?

Hannah We?

Cuttle No chance of me not coming.

Hannah You don't believe what I believe.

Cuttle I'll learn. I feel like a crusader. Not sure yet what I'm crusading about, but Lord, sir, I'll soon get the hang of it.

Hannah Billy, are you sure?

Cuttle I'm with you sir, no matter what.

Hannah I'm a god-damned woman, Billy, call me Hannah.

Cuttle Rot me, sir, I—ma'am, I—Lord, I'll try.

Godbolt WHEN YOU'VE DONE! There's not enough sail on her.

Hannah She'll do.

Godbolt Know it all, do you?

Hannah Enough.

Godbolt Grab my finger ends, Cuttle, before I throttle her.

Hannah Well, this is it. Goodbye, Susan. Goodbye my dear old land.

Cuttle And kippers and cider and Rosie by the pump that smells of cheese——

Godbolt Change your mind? Last chance.

Hannah Sooner ride a tiger with boils on my arse. There's a good wind blowing.

Cuttle It'll carry your words, ma'am. Blow 'em round the world. There. I said it. Ma'am.

Hannah It's close to midnight. We must go.

Godbolt What can you see on the horizon?

Hannah The flash of the sea.

Godbolt And then?

Hannah A star. A faint star.

Godbolt And furthest? On the rim?

Hannah Night.

Godbolt Hold to the star, Hannah.

Hannah I will, Godbolt. I will. This world must keep on turning, so it'll rain and it'll shine, the cows come to water and the pears fall in summer. On and on and on. UP HELM! LET EVERYTHING FLY!

The sail rises. Cuttle plays his whistle. As they sail off . . .

(*Calling back*) We won't settle for the dark.

Godbolt salutes. A star shines bright in the sky. Far away the wind blows

CURTAIN

FURNITURE AND PROPERTY LIST

The props listed below may be on stage throughout, with different areas of the stage being used for different scenes—see Production and Design Notes page xii. The Union Jack is prominently displayed throughout.

ACT I

The madhouse

On stage: Swing (see description page 1)
Oil-can for **Sculley**
Long-handled mop
Towel

Susan's house

On stage: Bed
Chair
Shelf. *On it:* letter, clock, mug, candles, matches, knife
Clothes chest. *In it:* shirt, long johns, stockings, shoes, cap, long piece of cloth, sock, jacket, trousers with kerchief in pocket

Personal: **Hannah:** locket

The dockyard

On stage: Board with ships' names
Drum, musket for **Drubber**
Book, pen for **Godbolt**

Off stage: Bundle **(Hannah)**
Uniforms (shirt, shoes, waistcoat, britches, coat, hat, bedding) for **Hannah** and **Cuttle (Stage Management)**
Load of muskets **(Drubber)**

Personal: **Drubber:** wig (required throughout)

The deck of the "Rainbow"

On stage: Mast, sail
Ropes, oars
Brooms, buckets of water and sand, holystone
Blankets
Cannon, cannon-balls

Off stage: Club, rations for the men (beer, biscuits), for himself (bread, pork, biscuits) **(Drubber)**
Rum **(Men)**
Glass **(Godbolt)**
Mallet **(Sculley)**
Spades, looted hat **(Crew)**

Personal: **Cuttle:** whistle (required throughout), knife, blood sacs
              Flegg: cheese, knife, kerchief
              Hannah: kerchief, letter, blood sacs, grapeshot

A small cove

On stage: Sand, rocks, driftwood, shells, stones
              Spades, bottle
              Piece of driftwood with enemy coat on it
              Remains of a body

Off stage: Shell **(Ditch)**

Personal: **Flegg:** apple in pocket

ACT II

The madhouse

On stage: As before

Personal: **Sculley:** handkerchief, comb and paper

Susan's house

On stage: Bed. *On it:* blanket, pillow
              Shelf. *On it:* note
              Chair. *On it:* shirt, skirt

An ante room

On stage: Table. *On it:* medals, papers
              Chair

Off stage: Petition **(Hannah)**
              One-man band (required for next few scenes) **(Cuttle)**

Personal: **Godbolt:** coins
              Cuttle: coins

A dressing-room

On stage: Chair. *On it:* **Hannah**'s uniform, **Cuttle**'s hat
              Sword, musket

On stage

On stage: Nil

Personal: **Hannah:** musket, sword (required for next few scenes)

The dressing-room

On stage: As before

Off stage: Thick official envelope **(Cumberland)**

On stage

On stage: Flags

The dressing-room

On stage: As before

Off stage: Torn flag

Personal: **Godbolt:** coin

On stage

On stage: Coin, book, chalk, pack of cards for **Godbolt**

Off stage: Night-dress, drum **(Sculleys)**
            Commitment papers **(Cumberland)**

The madhouse

On stage: As before, plus bowl of water

Off stage: Papers **(Kemp)**
            Keys **(Godbolt)**

The quayside

On stage: Small sailing boat with sail

LIGHTING PLOT

Property fittings required: nil

Various simple interior and exterior settings

ACT I

To open: Harsh light on **Hannah**

Cue 1	**Hannah** screams *Bring up lighting on madhouse*	(Page 1)
Cue 2	**Hannah:** "Oh, Davey ..." *Cross-fade to Susan's house*	(Page 2)
Cue 3	**Hannah** succeeds in whistling and is delighted *Cross-fade to dockyard*	(Page 5)
Cue 4	**Hannah** marches to join the others, followed by **Cuttle** *Cross-fade to deck of the "Rainbow"*	(Page 8)
Cue 5	**Hannah** is left with **Godbolt** *Change lighting to indicate ship is at sea*	(Page 10)
Cue 6	**Hannah** and **Cuttle** clasp hands *Pause, then fade lighting*	(Page 16)
Cue 7	The others join them *Return to previous lighting*	(Page 16)
Cue 8	Drums roll mightily, then die away *Fade lighting as darkness falls and men prepare for battle*	(Page 17)
Cue 9	**Flegg:** "Half-way to morning." *Gradually increase lighting*	(Page 20)
Cue 10	**Godbolt:** "HARD AS YOU CAN!" *Darkness, flashes, fire*	(Page 21)
Cue 11	Crew leave stage in the turmoil *Stop battle effects, lighting on* **Hannah** *and the* **Sculleys**	(Page 22)
Cue 12	The **Sculleys** exit *Increase lighting on deck of "Rainbow"*	(Page 22)
Cue 13	**Hannah** faints *Fade to lighting on* **Hannah**	(Page 25)
Cue 14	**Hannah:** "... a man's life all right." *Increase lighting*	(Page 26)
Cue 15	**All** (singing): "... but never made a king." *Cross-fade to small cove—warm, sunny lighting*	(Page 26)

| *Cue* 16 | **Hannah** (*a cry*): "NOWHERE!" | (Page 30) |
| | *Black-out* | |

ACT II

To open: Lighting on madhouse

| *Cue* 17 | The **Sculleys** exit | (Page 32) |
| | *Cross-fade to Susan's house* | |

| *Cue* 18 | **Hannah:** "To the Duke of Cumberland." | (Page 34) |
| | *Cross-fade to ante room* | |

| *Cue* 19 | **Hannah** marches off boldly, **Cuttle** follows | (Page 41) |
| | *Cross-fade to dressing-room* | |

| *Cue* 20 | **Godbolt:** "And don't forget to breathe." | (Page 42) |
| | *Cross-fade to on stage* | |

| *Cue* 21 | They bow and leave the stage | (Page 43) |
| | *Cross-fade to dressing-room* | |

| *Cue* 22 | **Hannah** marches out and on to the stage | (Page 45) |
| | *Cross-fade to on stage* | |

| *Cue* 23 | **Godbolt:** "The remarkable—HANNAH SNELL!" | (Page 45) |
| | *Increase lighting on stage* | |

| *Cue* 24 | Drum beats; wind blows | (Page 47) |
| | *Cross-fade to dressing-room* | |

| *Cue* 25 | **Godbolt:** "Right." | (Page 49) |
| | *Cross-fade to on stage—flashing lights, then spot on* **Godbolt** | |

| *Cue* 26 | **Godbolt:** "... the celebrated HANNAH SNELL." | (Page 50) |
| | *Spot on* **Hannah** | |

| *Cue* 27 | **Sculleys** force **Hannah** into night-dress | (Page 52) |
| | *Cut spots, increase lighting on madhouse* | |

| *Cue* 28 | **Sculley** sets swing in motion | (Page 54) |
| | *Bright lights on high end of swing* | |

| *Cue* 29 | The **Sculleys** exit | (Page 57) |
| | *Fade lighting* | |

| *Cue* 30 | **Hannah** finishes singing | (Page 57) |
| | *Increase lighting slightly* | |

| *Cue* 31 | The three stand linked a moment, then turn | (Page 60) |
| | *Lighting effect of water across stage* | |

| *Cue* 32 | They dive and swim through | (Page 60) |
| | *Gradually change lighting effect of water to sky and sea* | |

| *Cue* 33 | **Godbolt** salutes | (Page 61) |
| | *Star shines bright in the sky* | |

EFFECTS PLOT

ACT I

Cue 1   **Drubber** lets off musket shot   (Page 7)
Shot

Cue 2   **Hannah** and **Cuttle** finish dressing   (Page 8)
Drums

Cue 3   **Godbolt:** "LET EVERYTHING FLY!"   (Page 10)
Sail cracking

Cue 4   **Hannah** (calling down): "Ay ay."   (Page 12)
Flapping and cracking

Cue 5   **Hannah:** "NO! No, Drubber, STOP!"   (Page 15)
Wind blows mournfully

Cue 6   **Hannah:** "Sinking into the sea."   (Page 15)
Fade wind

Cue 7   **Cuttle:** "Shadow to shadow."   (Page 16)
Wind blows, throbbing beat begins

Cue 8   Stage darkens   (Page 16)
Wind blows hard, then fades; beat continues behind, then huge drum roll

Cue 9   **Godbolt:** "GOD SAVE THE KING!"   (Page 17)
Drums roll mightily, then die away

Cue 10   As they close in on one another   (Page 20)
Pipes sound

Cue 11   **Godbolt:** "MAKE SAIL!"   (Page 20)
Flapping, cracking of sails

Cue 12   **Godbolt:** "She's coming——"   (Page 21)
Boom of guns, bombardment shakes ship

Cue 13   **Goldbolt:** "STAND HARD AS DOGS!"   (Page 21)
Tremendous splintering crash, ship rocks, shrieks off

Cue 14   **Godbolt:** "She's almost on us."   (Page 21)
Another bombardment

Cue 15   **Godbolt:** "HARD AS YOU CAN!"   (Page 21)
Ship's guns fire, flashes, screams, fire

Cue 16   **Godbolt:** "He's no good dead."   (Page 22)
Battle rises to crescendo of sound and fury; huge tearing sound as sail comes crashing down

Cue 17   The **Sculleys** exit   (Page 22)
Smoke streams across stage

Cue 19   **Cuttle:** "There's nothing, sir." They dig   (Page 29)
         Beat begins

Cue 20   **Ditch:** "He's a heavy-arsed dog."   (Page 30)
         Beat becomes stronger

Cue 21   **Hannah:** "No. It's filled." They move   (Page 30)
         Wind

Cue 22   **Hannah** (a cry): "NOWHERE!"   (Page 30)
         Increase beat and wind

ACT II

Cue 23   As Lights come up on dressing-room   (Page 41)
         Music, rowdy crowd, off

Cue 24   **Godbolt:** "And don't forget to breathe."   (Page 42)
         Cut music; crowd in background

Cue 25   **Hannah** (singing): "More for love or glory do."   (Page 43)
         Applause—fade as Lights cross-fade to dressing-room

Cue 26   As Lights come up on dressing-room   (Page 43)
         Crowd noise, off

Cue 27   As Lights come up on stage   (Page 45)
         Fade crowd noise

Cue 28   **Godbolt:** "HANNAH SNELL!"   (Page 45)
         Music

Cue 29   **Hannah:** "That a woman bravely fought ..." (She falters)   (Page 46)
         Beat begins

Cue 30   They lurch off in disarray   (Page 46)
         *Boos from crowd, drum beats steadily, wind blows; fade as Lights
            come up on dressing-room*

Cue 31   **Hannah** gives correct time. **Godbolt:** "Is that correct?" (Page 51)
         Wind begins to blow

Cue 32   **Hannah:** "... greater than—darker than——"   (Page 51)
         Wind blows hard, then dies down

Cue 33   **Godbolt** salutes   (Page 61)
         Wind blows far away

MADE AND PRINTED IN GREAT BRITAIN BY
LATIMER TREND & COMPANY LTD PLYMOUTH

MADE IN ENGLAND